Norman
Here is
father wrote. He ____
and blessed life and I pray
that his legacy lives on
thru his children, grand-
children and great-grand-
children.

Sincerely
Sam Siph

The best is yet to come

By Martin Seppala
with Richard Drebert

Published in Beaverton, Oregon, by Good Book Publishing.
www.goodbookpublishing.com
V1.1

Printed in the United States of America

Table of Contents

Dedication

To my 17 gifted sons and daughters whom I treasure:
*Millie, Marci, Mindy, Josh, Amos, Heidi, Matt, Benny, Nate,
Joey, Wanda, Jon, Debbie, Sam, Annie, Sandy and Daniel.*

To my 9 beloved stepsons and stepdaughters, who have
delighted me every day since my wedding to Nancy:
Norma, Janie, Aly, John, Steve, Dave, Rod, Naomi and Bruce.

To our 130 spirited grandchildren,
who inspire us to think and act young.

To our great-grandchildren,
some born, and others to follow.

And to our one great-great-grandchild
(and every future one to come!).

May all of you seek and find the Way, the Truth and the Life.
I savor a marvelous contentment knowing that my sins are
forgiven by the cleansing blood of Jesus. It's my sincere prayer
that every soul on earth experience the security and joy of
knowing Jesus. Faith in Christ guarantees peace for eternity.

Acknowledgements

First and foremost, my heart overflows with gratitude for my wife, Nancy, who kept our "literary summit" in sight as we scaled the mountain of memories together. Without her adventurous spirit, foresight and guidance, my scribbled thoughts would be gathering cobwebs in some closet. Nancy's love for me is bound to every word in *The Best Is Yet To Come*. Her insights and mine are expressed as one, for readers to ponder as they navigate life.

I shared laughter and tears with Richard Drebert, the Christian writer who forged events (spanning more than a century) into an engaging story of my ancestry and life. With each in-depth interview, we grew to love Richard more. We value our future relationship with him and his family.

Good Book Publishing Project Manager, Jane Petrick, shepherded our project to completion with top-notch editing skills, scheduling and care for details. Jane is a joy to work with, and her warm regard for Nancy and I made our book journey a wonderful experience.

May God reward my brothers, sisters, aunts, uncles, grandparents and extended family who influenced me to serve Jesus my whole life. I acknowledge those faithful Christians that God used to shape my character: preachers, teachers and families of the Apostolic Lutheran Church. Many of these were business associates — men just as comfortable nailing a top plate to a stud wall as shuffling contracts in a boardroom.

Finally, I reserve unique admiration for my parents, Gus and Annie Seppala, who showed me how to love unconditionally. By my father's daily example, he instilled the strong Finnish work ethic that set me on the path to prosperity. Mother's Godly lifestyle taught me to prize my Christian faith far above every ambition I have ever pursued.

Introduction

Many people have come to me asking me to write a book, knowing that I have lived a very active and eventful life. I decided I would try to portray my life story in this book hoping my posterity and friends would find their way to the fulfilled and joyous life that has blessed me. Born before television, computers and wireless phones, I have experienced a lot of changes in life. The things that have never changed were taught in my childhood home.

My prayer is that none would perish and all would be saved. There is only one way to be truly happy, and I hope you, the reader of this book, will find this pathway and plant your feet firmly on it.

"The joy of the Lord is your strength" (Nehemiah 8:10).

"Whosoever liveth and believeth in me shall never die" (John 11:26).

I hope this book will inspire you to search out the secrets of happiness and get direction and hope for your future. The best is yet to come!

Seppala family tree

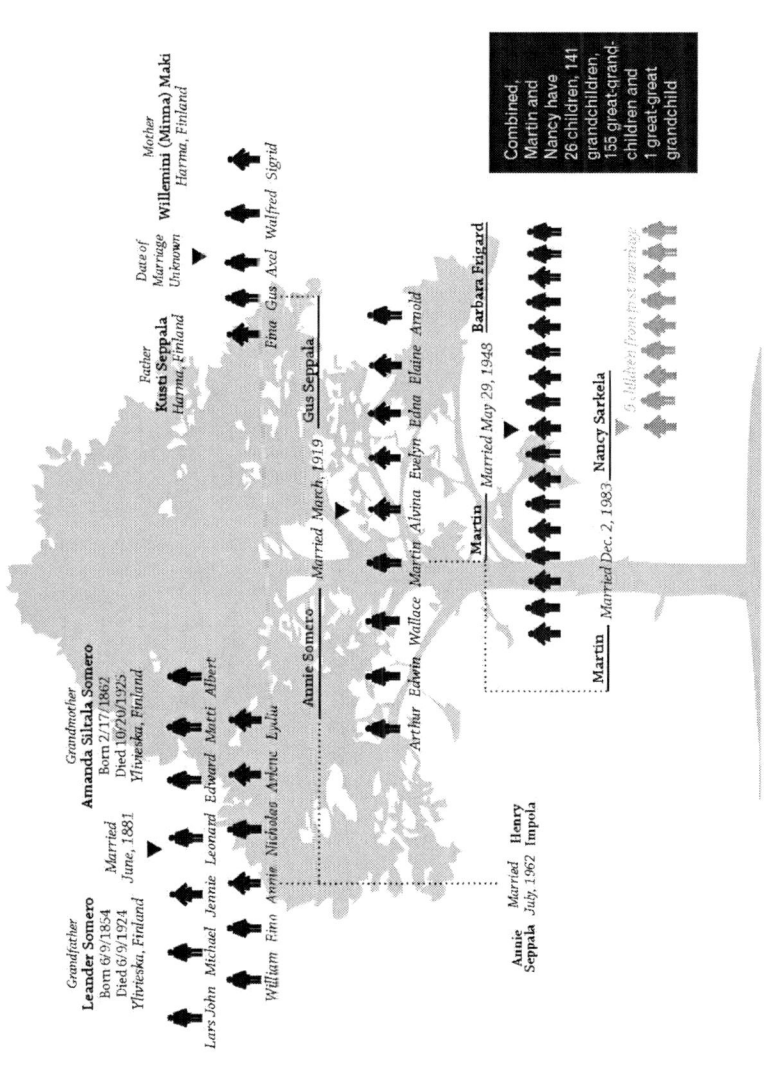

Combined, Martin and Nancy have 26 children, 141 grandchildren, 155 great-grandchildren and 1 great-great grandchild

Chapter one
Roots of ambition

In the Number 5 coal tunnel, Gus Seppala felt the black dust shift under his boots. From the belly of the mine, a dynamite charge rumbled like fading thunder as he trudged outside, squinting into the evening sun. Chinese laborers stood aside as he passed, picks and shovels on shoulders, ready to bear away the coal and debris cast from the blast. After the Chinese finished their work, Gus and a crew of Finnish carpenters would shore up the tunnel with heavy timbers to extend the narrow gauge rails for coal cars.

None of the Chinese even glanced at the departing miners. Not many years before, at the Rock Springs mine, ethnic hatred had boiled over, and mineworkers had murdered one another over wages.

Today Gus was just glad to be *working*. It wouldn't be long before he abandoned rock drills and dynamite forever. He smiled into a blessed Wyoming breeze, thinking of his wife and little Gus snug in their miner's cabin ... and about supper.

Potatoes and beef!

Back in Finland, his father never let him forget "the great hunger years" in 1866-1868. Lakes and rivers around their home village of Harma had stayed frozen until nearly June. Then a scant summer growing season and an early September frost ravaged the potato harvest. By midwinter, the stores of grain had run out all over Finland. Beggars filled the streets of Helsinki and farm villages alike. The famine lasted three years, and 270,000 died of starvation. Disease swept the country. Those three years had demoralized a generation.

In 1888, Gus, Amanda and little Gus Seppala left the glut of

The best is yet to come

jobless laborers in Finland to board a crowded steamship sailing for America. Little Gus' father knew that unrest swelled among working class Finns like a pot of wheat simmering over a fire. By the thousands, disillusioned families were deserting their homeland. Russian Czar Alexander III reckoned these "subjects" as disloyal to his royal patronage: The Czar regarded himself as the "Grand Duke of Finland."

Gus had squirreled away enough money for ship fares, and his family of three had braved weeks of seasickness to finally land in America, looking like bedraggled migrating ducks. They boarded the Union Pacific Railroad jolting across the country for days until arriving at Rock Springs, Wyoming, where no celestial hymn ever sounded sweeter than their native Suomi tongue spoken by Finnish miners.

Finnish neighbors had constructed common saunas for their families, and the Seppalas settled into a routine seldom enjoyed back home in Harma: full bellies at bedtime and the security of work every day. But before a year had passed, Gus already mapped out a plan to move east.

He would work in the coal mines long enough to save up for a farm. He had heard of fertile farmland in a Finnish community called Westminster, Massachusetts, and the cities in the East hired men with his skills: mechanics, carpentry, farming. Besides, he could learn *anything*.

☙☙☙☙

Leander Somero sucked in a final clean draught of air before the stench of pulverized ore consumed him again. Helmet candles cast eerie shadows against the rock walls as the "man car," conveying 30 men, clattered deep into the gloom of the copper mine. He had been working in these dirty throats for the Calumet and Hecla Company for 10 years, since the days when everyone called the little town of Calumet "Red Jacket."

Roots of ambition

Leander and his wife, Minna, lived outside of Calumet in a house too small for his growing family. *Restlessness*, like a wild friend from his youth, stirred his soul. This adventurous stirring had called to his nature in Finland, when he had left Minna and their baby, John, in Ylivieska.

Leander had sailed to America with his two brothers and pounded out steamship fares at the copper mine, bringing his family to Michigan after two lonely years. He was a farmer at his core, but the copper mines provided him a foothold in America and roots in a community with brethren who had fled the poverty of Finland.

And like him, these poor Finnish immigrants had carried the message of "forgiveness of sins in Jesus' name and the blood" as the core of their reformed Lutheran faith, faith tethered like an anchor to the sweeping Nordic revival of the 1840s. A strong adherence to the principles in the Bible during times of trial had kept these Christian communities together through "the great hunger years." Now those same Godly principles enhanced a rich Finnish culture in America.

From his youth, Leander nurtured an ambition to create a working farm for his family, and finally his hope was materializing. Through the reliable Finnish grapevine, he found a farm for sale in New Ipswich, New Hampshire. Leander and Minna planned to break ground in a new community. He had dodged cave-ins, dashed from short fuses and evaded rockslides for too long in the Michigan copper mines. Now was time for a new season.

Leander shut out the murmur of miners around him as they marched down the tunnel like an army of ants. He prayed, "God, please bless our family as we move to New Hampshire," and within the warren of darkness, Leander's heart glowed with God's approval.

৵৵৵

The best is yet to come

Two ambitious immigrants, Leander Somero and Gus Seppala, left mine dust and rock drills behind them and bought farmland in the Northeastern United States. Neither man had more than an elementary school education. But with true-hearted wives they would raise 17 children between them, create homes for their families and become respected men in their communities.

On separate tracks, these Finnish families gathered steam until joined in a blessed union borne in the wedlock of a faithful daughter and ambitious son.

৵৵৵

It was hard to ignore Gus Seppala. Annie Somero lost count as she sorted a batch of 5,000 shoe tacks. The handsome dark-haired Finn grinned at her as she glanced away. Annie worked hard every day at the Granite State Tack Company, then rode with her brothers five miles home to the Somero family farm at New Ipswich.

Months had gone by since she told one of the Gransfors boys (who had left to fight in the trenches of Europe) that she would wait for him. But that was before *Gus*. She could barely keep herself from tumbling head over heels for this cocky Finn, who never went to church.

Gus lived in Jaffrey, but he said that his family lived in Westminster, across the border in Massachusetts. At lunchtimes they had begun to sit together, Finns of a feather, speaking their native tongue, comparing families and heritages.

"I have two brothers and two sisters," Gus told her one day, and Annie smirked a little.

"I have 12!" It felt good to one-up Gus. "Nine brothers and three sisters! And when I have my *own* children someday, we shall all meet Jesus together on the resurrection morning."

Annie seemed distant for a moment, and Gus frowned a

little, feeling unusually thoughtful. Her frankness had touched his heart.

Annie smiled reassuringly. "I have a big, wonderful family, Gus," she said.

"I should like to meet them."

His directness and the warmth in his voice made her look away.

"Then you should come to our church, Gus Seppala."

"Hmmm. I might just do that."

"You'll have to, if you want to meet my father."

And he *did* come.

Gus Seppala drove his Model A Ford along Poor Farm Road in New Ipswich, a few miles south of Jaffrey, then pulled into a small gravel parking lot hemmed in by massive pines and maples. He slammed the car door a little too hard, and a few brawny men in suits stared at him from the church steps. A sharp steeple above the doorway pierced the heavens, and he took a deep breath, like he was about to run a footrace.

The Somero girl inhabited most of his waking moments *and* his dreams these days. He reminded himself why he was visiting the little white Apostolic Lutheran Church.

It *was* about Annie, wasn't it?

A few friendly people greeted him at the doors in Finnish (Suomea), and inside he spotted Annie in a blue and white dress sitting between a stocky man with sandy hair and an attractive middle-aged woman, obviously her mother. What seemed like rows and rows of Someros greeted him, and at the end of the line, he shook Leander Somero's beefy hand. Gus met Annie's father's gaze, man to man, and Leander *smiled.* Gus would value that intense, approving smile for as long as the elder Somero lived.

Before the service began, thumping sounds in the back of the church captured Gus' attention, and he grinned at a herd of boys and girls playing in the high balcony. In fact, babies and toddlers and boys and girls seemed to be romping in every corner of the little church.

By the end of the pastor's message, preached in Finnish, Gus Seppala knew that his visit had been meant to happen, and it *wasn't* just about Annie. He drove away from the church musing about the genuineness he felt among these men and women. These were his people, but a force stronger than culture drew him.

"You come back, son," Leander had said, and the invitation had lodged deep in his soul.

On the next Sunday, he hadn't planned to partake of the Lord's Supper. But after the sermon on John 20:23, he rose with the rest of the congregation and knelt at the altar, thinking hard about his life.

Beside him, two elderly friends embraced and mended fences over past wrongs, weeping. Others humbly reached their arms to clasp the pastor's neck as they received forgiveness and individually partook of the body and blood of Jesus, the bread and wine.

Gus reflected on the preacher's sermon:

The blood of Christ has paid for your sins. To receive eternal life, ask God to forgive you. Clear all accounts you hold against others, and restore relationships with those you know you have offended.

The pastor bent close. Gus clasped his neck with a strong arm and confessed his sins, welcoming the man's words, like they came from the mouth of God himself: "All your sins are forgiven in the name and blood of Jesus." Unexpected tears fell like a steady drizzle, and it seemed like Gus breathed clean air for the first time.

Annie studied the young man kneeling at the altar, sorting out her own feelings. She was aware of the Gransfors and worried a little about what they were thinking. It was obvious to everyone that Gus and Annie were *friendly*, and God had suddenly changed everything. Gus Seppala was what the Bible called a "new creation," and his smile was different when he looked her way. His happiness now seemed to come from his heart, and not just his head.

In the months that followed, their lunches together at the tack factory became more and more meaningful. Gus courted Annie with propriety and spent time with the Someros. Annie loved the Seppalas from the start, and her marriage to Gus set the families on a single track powered by the blessings of God.

ॐॐॐ

Anyone in attendance at my 1st birthday on January 14, 1926 would have sensed a bittersweet thanksgiving in my parents that evening. I was a long, hard labor of love for my mother, and when I finally arrived, the doctor's forceps gouged one eye during my delivery. Liquor on the doctor's breath told a sad story, and this eye tended to wander its own way for my entire childhood.

"Stop looking cross-eyed at us!" my brothers often teased me. But as I grew older, I knew that Jesus guided me with a superior lens for his purposes, even if I *was* legally blind in my left eye. Now, as I look back, I glory in this first trial, minutes before I was snuggling into my mother's loving arms.

I spent my first years growing up in Jaffrey, New Hampshire. Then we moved to my parents' lifetime home in Rindge. And during my entire childhood, Gus and Annie Seppala never allowed little Marty to indulge in a moment of self-pity.

By my 3rd birthday, Dad quit the Granite State Tack Company and grabbed the gearshift of a dual-axle truck at NETCO, the New England Truck Company. He drove the rigs and repaired them, making himself indispensible to George Todd, the road agent at Rindge.

The best is yet to come

The Great Depression hit around 1929. Many of our neighbors in New Hampshire lost their jobs, and the elders in our churches warned that famine might be stalking the Finnish people again. But America had a government and resources that Finland never dreamed of.

Dad worked throughout the Depression driving for NETCO and even bought a small house with 4 acres on Payson Hill Road. We lived a quarter-mile from Rindge Common, the city's center.

Dad and Mom called their two-room home the "camp," and it was an eyesore to the community of Rindge with its picture-perfect Congregational Church (used as the town hall), Fuller's Store and a two-story schoolhouse huddled cozily next to the music teacher's home. Payson Hill Road ran right between the church and the school and continued past our "camp." On the outskirts of town, sawmills roared day and night, and at repair shops, mechanics and welders in greasy overalls talked over politics and engines and crop prices.

My little sister Alvina was born while we lived at the "camp" — one big living room/kitchen and one bedroom. At the beginning of the Depression, Dad decided to have our new house built, and he set a dizzying pace for us to follow. As soon as Mother finished serving up supper, he headed out the door to shovel out a hole 70 feet from the dirt roadway. Gathering rocks for groundwork became a family chore, and Dad only put down his shovel and pick after digging the basement 24 feet wide and 28 feet long. Matti and Emanual Aho, men from our Apostolic Lutheran Church congregation, framed the house on the stone foundation Dad laid.

I was 4 years old when we moved into the house in 1930, and I ran wild in our two big bedrooms upstairs, plus a spacious bedroom and a living room/kitchen downstairs. Dad's total cost for construction: a whopping $1,000!

But Dad wasn't happy with his wife "running

water" (literally) from a hand pump to the house. So he dug a new well, piped the water to the kitchen and bathroom and installed a Sears, Roebuck and Co. pump. He dug a hole for a septic crib, and behold! We did away with the two-holer outhouse. Annie Seppala had to whittle down her pride before Sunday services when friends asked how she liked her new home. Her husband had provided amenities that folks in the city had!

My father was just as innovative at work as he was at his family farm. In the 20s and 30s, hand scythes or horse-drawn mowers cut the thick rye or vetch in the hayfields or thistly weeds in public right-of-ways. Don Eaves repaired and welded equipment for the local folk, and Dad mulled over a design in his head for a mower run by a power takeoff and mounted on a vehicle. One day he drug an old horse-drawn mower to Don's shop along with a Model A Ford, and he and the old mechanic set to work whacking up car body and shortening the wheel base. Dad and Don geared up a power takeoff for the driveshaft and set up a mower blade near the driver's seat to be raised and lowered. Their new grass mower worked like a champ for the city of Rindge and farming neighbors for years and years.

కాకాకా

"Mr. Martin's here!"

I hollered like a Viking raider and danced around the legs of Frank's two unflappable draft mares. Every spring Frank harrowed Mom's garden for us, and I couldn't wait for him to start plowing on this fine morning. Frank tipped his hat to my mother and drove his matched mares to our 1-acre garden plot.

"Marty! Keep out of Mr. Martin's way!"

I fell in behind the team, kicking dirt clods with bare feet, and Frank took a deep breath, preparing himself …

"So, Mr. Martin? Why do horses go so slow?"

The best is yet to come

"'Cause the plow's heavy, Marty."

"I wonder *why*? And how do they know where to go?"

"See these reins, son?"

"Hmmm. I wonder *why*? Do you like your horses?"

"Yeeees …"

"I wonder *why*, Mr. Martin?"

And so it went for hours. Frank and his horses turned the earth for our garden. Little did he know that his good nature plowed and planted patience in my fertile mind, and in years to come, I remembered his forbearance when dealing with my own 17 children.

"Gus, I call your Marty the 'Wonder Boy,'" Frank chuckled, and the name stuck to me like pitch on a shoe.

My dad had other names for me, and every one of them made me feel special, like Punkin' Head or Chubby. On nights he drove his plow truck to clear snow for the city, I begged to ride along. He often took me as company to keep him awake, but I always dropped off to sleep against his burly shoulder.

Building a Finnish work ethic into my brain became a full-time job for my parents, and I dreaded my commander's deep growl before he went to work in the summertime: "Today, you boys weed the garden."

To this day, I muse, "Oh, Adam! Why did you have to eat that forbidden fruit?"

కళళ

Three cultural distinctions set Finns apart in America: their Lutheran roots, their Finnish language and their *saunas*.

Dad beveled logs to form a tight siding for our sauna, and no smoke leaked into our steam room because my father built it according to his special design. A chimney carried the fumes outside from a firebox made of stone and brick. It was our custom for my parents to build a fire on Saturdays inside this firebox, and it heated water in a 55-gallon drum. When a pile of stones placed atop the firebox grew red hot, we dipped hot water from the drum and doused them to produce a pore-cleansing steam, with temperatures as high as 200 degrees. Of course, children and stoves sometimes added up to trouble.

Mother had sent four of us boys out to have our sauna baths, and my brother Arthur tossed a dipper of hot water onto the cold seats to warm them. I hopped off the top bench to avoid a scalding and somehow ended up on the lid of the 55-gallon barrel of boiling water. The lid tipped, and my foot slid inside!

I lit out across the snow-covered yard, limping, screaming to Mom, and she enfolded me in a blanket to calm me. She disappeared outside for a time and came back with an ancient remedy for burns, used for generations back in Finland. In a towel, Mom caked a generous portion of fresh cow manure, and she bound my foot inside as I cried. I don't recall how long I had to wear my dung bandage, but it seemed to draw the heat from the burn.

Before my family had a sauna available, it was our custom to visit relatives who had one, for example, Nick Somero, my mother's brother. It became a weekly social event: Women with girls took their turns first, then the men with boys sat inside on the hardwood benches. Everyone rinsed off with cool water after "cooking" for a time. Then the cousins ran wild everywhere, playing late into the evening, while parents drank coffee and talked about life.

߬߬߬

"Tattletale, tattletale, hanging on a cow's big tail! When the cow begins to pee, YOU will have a cup of TEA!"

My brother Wally was a year and a half older than I was, and we were best friends, partners in mischief. Arthur was five years older than I was and our self-appointed watchdog. But when he reported our escapades to Mother (like chucking rocks at a neighbor girl), it could easily sentence us to a good hair yank or two.

Our barn held stalls enough for 10 milk cows, and over the years, Dad added a grain silo and milking room with a cooler to keep the milk fresh. Laying hens squawked and roosters crowed early mornings as we kids gathered eggs. We fed the cows and mixed scraps into a sloppy brew for the hogs.

When our grain and pig feed ran low, Dad made a trip to town. "Get plenty of the same flowered designs, Gus," Mom instructed, and my father waved and nodded as he drove away. His weekly jaunt to the feed store doubled as fabric shopping in a roundabout way. Dad bought grain in bags made of cotton. Each bag was stamped with beautiful colored patterns, and Mother used these livestock, pig and chicken feed sacks as "fabric" to sew up beautiful dresses for my sisters or sheets and pillowcases for our beds.

Locally, Mom was known as a wonderful seamstress. She made most of the clothing for us kids, especially when we were young. One day a neighbor asked Mom to create a coat for her daughter, and in a week, the woman picked up the beautiful garment. Alvina's cherub-like face beamed as the woman complimented the wonderful stitching, and suddenly the neighbor placed a dime in the child's hand, just to be friendly.

"And how much do I owe you, Annie?"

"Not a thing. I wouldn't think of it," Mom said. But the woman then placed another 50 cents in Alvina's little hand.

"Alvina's got 60 cents!" I whispered to Wally, and after Mom's friend left, we took our little sister by the hand and kindly escorted her to Fuller's Store in Rindge.

Honey dripped from our lips as we politely ordered up a bag of red, green, blue and orange lollipops, hard candy and black licorice, until every penny was gone.

Roots of ambition

"Thank you, Mr. Fuller."

We were almost bowing as we left his store, dragging Alvina with us. Not far from home, heavy rollers were stowed in a tin shed that was dug into a hillside. Horses pulled these rollers on the streets in winter, to pack down snow so folks could travel along easier by foot.

By now, our consciences were smarting over duping our innocent little sister, but not yet enough to send us home to repent. We chose "sin for a season," and climbed up the hill above the roller shed and settled down to gorge atop our own "big rock candy mountain."

I stopped chewing for just a few seconds when I spotted Arthur, who had spotted us. We didn't offer Arthur a single bite as he read us the riot act on our way home to justice. Mom had sent Arthur to find Alvina and collect the 60 cents she carried.

It was *way* too late for that.

I cannot recall my mother's face ever looking so red or her words sounding so loud as when she spoke to Mr. Fuller on the phone. All I remember of her conversation with the storekeeper was how he should have "known better than to sell all that candy to little kids" and how in "these hard times 60 cents could have bought a lot of bread." I was grateful that Mom's wrath was directed away from me, but I still had to reckon with my father.

Mom seldom spanked her children. Her nature was as sweet as peaches, and she loved to join in games and water fights with us. It was her job to buy all the Christmas gifts each year, and she usually took Arthur with her to help. Sometimes Wally and I shared one gift, which was fine with us since we played together, anyway. Wally and I knew where Arthur hid the presents before Santa Claus "delivered" them, and we snuck into the barn to dig under the hay. It was great fun to discover everyone's gifts before they were presented and then act surprised.

The best is yet to come

It was through Mom that a deep yearning to know Jesus settled in my little soul. Some of my best memories are waking up on her lap at our New Ipswich church, secure with family and friends, with songs about Zion echoing in the sanctuary. At home my mother sang about Jesus often as she sat in her wooden rocker. I lay on the floor beside her, steeped in her gentleness and longing to see heaven, too.

My mother never bought a single book on how to discipline boys or raise her girls; she simply applied common sense and Bible principles as she steered us into a structured Christian culture. My parents surrounded us with other good men and women to emulate, and we loved it because we knew of no other way to live.

Mom and Dad instilled within us an independent spiritual heritage that took root during my childhood. To this day my heart's desire is to be a child of God, believing and trusting in the work of Jesus, who bore my sins and the sins of the whole world. Jesus willingly shed his blood which became the atonement for anyone who believes and trusts him.

As long as she lived, Mom reminded us: "I pray for you, so that you remain in the faith all the days of your life. On that great resurrection morning, I'll say to Jesus, 'See! I'm here with all my children that you have given me!'"

Now, as a scarred-up old soldier from life's battles, I can hardly wait for that beautiful resurrection morning in heaven where my mother waits. And I look forward to presenting my own children and grandchildren to Jesus, too.

❧ ❧ ❧

It began when I was 4 and a half years old, this drive to excel against all odds. My brother Wally was starting first grade, and I was indignant.

"Mom, why can't I go, too? I'll work hard. I can do it!"

Roots of ambition

It took a little convincing before she relented and talked to the teacher.

Miss Conner was reluctant but friendly. "We'll try him for one week. If he can keep up with the class, I'll accept him."

I followed Wally up the steps of my new school and began to think about how big everything seemed. I stared out the windows at the Rindge streets and trees and birds ... then Miss Conner asked me to sit in a circle of chairs with the other students.

"We shall begin with reciting the alphabet, children."

My mind darted everywhere, except on the teacher and her lesson. *I think I shall look at the ceiling. No, I think I will look at the floor, now.*

After a few attempts to corral my concentration, Miss Collins gave up. She sent me home to Mom for another year.

ॐॐॐ

As a child, I had no idea that I shared my stomping grounds with famous people. Writers Ralph Waldo Emerson, Henry David Thoreau and Rudyard Kipling had tramped the woods at Monadnock, a 2,000-foot mountain north of Rindge. Standing outside our sauna, we could see Monadnock, the grandest peak in Cheshire County. Mark Twain had visited the region, too, and I think he might have found inspiration for some of his stories had he known *me* as a boy.

Yet, surpassing any famous folk around Rindge or Jaffrey or New Ipswich, I cherished my uncle Bill, Mom's older brother, who had a cottage in New Ipswich. He often drove to visit us, and I loved to hear his old Model A Ford puttering into the yard. Bill was a trusted man who helped us impressionable nieces and nephews, and my special trip to Jaffrey with my uncle pointed to ambitions percolating deep in boyish dreams.

The best is yet to come

"Anybody want to go with me to pick up some lumber?"

"You betcha!"

I glanced at Mom's face, and she nodded over her sewing. Alvina and Evelyn were preoccupied with dolls, and I hopped into the Model A beside my uncle, thrilled! For miles and miles I would have his undivided attention. So many subjects, and so little time: questions about his car, the weather, hunting …

The best thing about Uncle Bill was that he really listened. "I'm goin' to build things, and I'll have a big company and 'bout 300 trucks!"

"Three hundred, you say?"

"Yup!"

We'd been driving for several minutes, and the Model A sputtered once, jerked and stalled. Bill looked a little disgusted with himself.

"We're out of gas, Marty." He steered off the road and flung open his door. "You ready for a hike?"

"Yup!"

This trip was getting better all the time. I picked up a rock and skipped it across Pool Pond as we walked by. "Boy, it's a good thing the other kids didn't come with us, huh, Uncle Bill?"

Not far from Pool Pond a neighbor gave us a lift to the store for a can of gas. At the supper table that night, Bill talked about our trip. "Your boy has drive, Gus, and I think he really just might end up with his 300 trucks."

Like an essential gear in Dad's truck, Uncle Bill was important to our family. He never did find the right woman to marry, but it seemed to suit him fine.

❧❧❧

I began attending classes officially the year following my first distracted try at academics. Mother kissed my forehead and admonished me to mind the teacher as I ran to catch up with

Roots of ambition

Wally, a "veteran" student by now. All the way to school, he thoroughly educated me on what I could NOT get away with in class.

A smiling Miss Collins assigned me a magnificent desk, constructed of black iron and hardwood, with a single storage shelf beneath a scuffed top and an inkwell in the upper corner. Forty desks faced a blackboard with two words neatly chalked across the top: "Miss Collins." But I couldn't have cared less about the scribbling; I was busy examining my fellow pupils seated around me.

They ranged from first to sixth grade, and we all sat in one large room with tall paned windows and dull white walls. Two closed doors shut off smaller rooms.

Miss Collins taught eight students at my first-grade level, a sprinkling of second- and third-graders, a smattering of fourth and fifth and a healthy dash of sixth-graders. Above us, on the second floor, the seventh- and eighth-grade students studied with another teacher, Miss Youngquest. In the 1930s, the town of Rindge only hired teachers who were unmarried.

Beneath our desks, in a finished basement, the wood-fired furnace belched heat through vents in the floors, warming us during the bitter New Hampshire winters. The furnace shared the basement with a four-holer toilet reserved for female teachers and students. Another enclosed four-holer adorned the side of the school, just *outside* of the basement. Our janitor regularly shoveled lime into the facilities to keep the smell from overpowering us.

In the first 15 minutes of the new school year, Miss Collins explained the essential classroom code for using the bathroom facilities during class. One finger up: number one, entitling the student to a *very* short desk vacancy. Two fingers up: number two, acceptable for a longer duration away. I was way ahead of Miss Collins; I had learned the toilet code from Wally at one of *his* lectures.

The best is yet to come

Wally and I ran home from school for lunch, and I couldn't wait to recount my terrific first hours of learning new things to Mom. She always welcomed my stories like great literature, and her encouragement and interest in my childhood pursuits equipped me to venture far from my comfort zones over and over in life. Unlike our public schools today, my mother could be certain that the foundation of every subject I studied for the next several years agreed with the enduring principles from the Bible she taught at home.

If students lived within one mile of school, they walked. A school bus picked up children who lived farther away. At precisely 9 a.m., we all answered the teacher's melodious brass bell, swung with a wooden handle, and marched promptly to stand by the desks assigned us for the whole year.

"Our Father, who art in heaven, hallowed be thy name ..." The Lord's Prayer set the tone for reading, language and arithmetic, for students and teachers alike.

"Ready. Salute: 'I pledge allegiance to the flag, of the United States of America ...'"

Recess!

We had two every day, and when they came, we scrambled out the door as fast as we could, not wasting a second of the free time.

Girls played hopscotch, and boys crowded around circles scratched into the ground for "bunny in the hole," a game of skill and chance with marbles. Girls and boys often played baseball together, but few of us had mitts. We brought our own equipment from home, since the school board never believed sports to be a vital part of our education. A catcher's mitt, however, did show up one year, purchased by the school, to relieve the catcher of sore hands.

During the first snow, usually in November, we bundled up like Eskimos: woolen coats and stockings, long johns and hats with flaps or earmuffs. Every kind of sled imaginable came out of barns or from under porches. But most often we just shared pieces of cardboard to careen down a hill in front of the school. The slick icy layer on the bottom of the cardboard would last for days.

However, often a few of us never made it out for recess at all. Our teachers adhered to a strict set of rules that our parents affirmed with added severity. No one talked during class, except when called upon after a raised hand. The teacher weighed the merits of every class interruption: requests to sharpen a pencil, get a drink or ask a question. If declared inappropriate, a recess might be forfeited, or worse, a paddling might be administered.

Every day a seventh- or eighth-grade boy was entrusted a job that took him out of school and down the street to Rindge's town water pump, and I couldn't wait to be old enough. This favored son carried water back to the schoolroom and filled a 2-gallon water pot. A single cup hung from the wall, and during the day, students and teachers drank from the same cup whenever they were thirsty.

After the last frost of the year, a stretch of sunshine set Mom on a tear to get the garden planted once Mr. Martin turned the soil. Calves and piglets filled our pens, chicks hatched and the whole county seemed to be working to prepare for harvest time.

Barefoot, finally!

After school closed for summer break, Wally, shoeless, promptly hopped onto a nail in back of the barn. Dad sat Wally down, cleansed his puncture and sent him off to play again. Emergencies always sent us wailing to find our "doctor." Our parents handled most injuries unless they judged our wound serious enough to cause permanent damage. As summer wore on, our feet toughened like shoe leather, and the only time we wore shoes was on Sunday morning for church.

Mom reached beyond our farm to supplement Dad's income, and she stirred up the "gifts" she read in her children's personalities. When I was 8, Mom drafted me to test my business skills.

"Marty, Mr. Rice is the richest man in Rindge, and he isn't using his pasture. Go rent it from him." I could see the excitement in her eyes. "We'll harvest the blueberries there."

I stoked up my courage and knocked on Harris Rice's door. The man was very gracious as I negotiated a rental agreement. We sealed the deal with a handshake, and our relationship continued for many years.

I had no idea how much work blueberry picking was when I shook hands that morning, but at the end of summer, I found out. Arthur was 16 at the time, and all of us kids piled into the car with Mom as he drove us to harvest wild blueberries. It took forever to fill one crate with 32 quarts of tiny blue fruit, but the stores in Boston purchased all that Mom could supply.

Before winter hit again, Mom would take out the Spiegel catalogue and pick out clothing for the school year: two bib overalls, two long-sleeved shirts and underwear for each boy. When the clothing arrived, we boys couldn't wait to rip open our packages, postmarked *Chicago.*

But Mom wouldn't let us wear anything until school. On the first day of school, I marched to my desk proud as a stiff peacock in my spankin' new clothes, bought with our blueberry money. All school year, we boys wore one set of bibs and a shirt all week, while Mom and the girls washed the other.

そそそ

At 8 years old, my forceful personality began cropping up in all sorts of ways. One day, I walked over to my friend Wayne's house and was disappointed when he wasn't home. But a delightful hubbub across the road invited investigation: An auctioneer stood on a stump calling out bids and prices.

"What's my bid on this fine garden rake?"

Roots of ambition

I felt a nickel in my pocket and fished it out. "Five cents!"

The auctioneer ignored me, but the clutch of men around him chuckled, and someone bought the rake.

"Bidding on this wheelbarrow begins at …"

"A nickel!" I shouted and followed up every item on the block, from sheep shears to harrows, with my same 5-cent bid.

Suddenly, the auctioneer surprised me. "Sold for a nickel, to the young man in the front there!"

He handed me a clock with a brass pendulum that was nearly as tall as me, and I carried it away proudly, though halfway home I struggled with buyer's remorse, it was so heavy. And I'm sure the auctioneer was glad I was gone.

రీఎం రీఎం రీఎం

A dentist showed up one day at school to offer his services to the "poor" children of the community. The Depression took a bite out of most Rindge families' budgets, and teeth were the one thing that even my dad couldn't repair with his tools.

My first experience with this dentist is still vivid in my mind.

From my school desk, I could see an eerie light glowing from an open door to a small room where a white-knuckled friend gripped the sides of a wooden chair. The boy's mouth gaped open, and a bucket sat on a table beside him where a big man tromped on a foot pedal powering a whirring drill.

"Open wider, son!" The patient groaned as the dentist's instrument descended.

Words in my reading book ran together in a blur. The horror show ended, and my friend stumbled out of the room, holding his jaw.

"Next, Martin Seppala …"

Panic.

I was a good Christian boy, and I dutifully entered the

chamber and sat. But that's when my sinful nature took control.

"Sir, my mother said NOT to do anything to my teeth but clean them!"

Somehow the surly dentist read between the lines of my whopper, and he looked grouchy, like I had spit on his charity.

"Out! Home with you. Next ..."

I never fessed up to Mom. She would have felt terrible about my lie. Decades later, I was speaking to someone, pretty proudly, that I couldn't recall a time when I had told an out-and-out lie. Suddenly, the Holy Spirit ran this whole episode across the screen of my mind.

Oops.

It sure confirmed the scriptures. I knew about sin. A sin nature really does live in me, and I must examine my heart daily. Jesus' blood cleanses me, but I bear a responsibility to confess sin to God and keep my relationship with him unencumbered.

෨෧෨෧෨෧

When I was in elementary school, my brother Edwin, three and a half years older than me, stood tall in my mind. He could create something useful from anything and demonstrated this gift when he grabbed a defective wooden barrel from the barn and built a wonderful sled. He smoothed the staves first, then fastened 2x4s as braces and a seat. We called it "the jumper," for obvious reasons, and blasted down steep hills smoothed by this curious-looking bobsled. Staying aboard the whole distance down the hill without tumbling into a drift showcased our supreme balance and skill.

With local ponds and lakes frozen thick, we clamped skates onto the bottoms of our shoes and braced for a season of concussions and bruises. Often the soles of our shoes peeled right off due to the cold leather twisting apart. Our ponds were like spacious sports arenas, and we built giant bonfires to keep warm and roast potatoes. Edwin always took time to help us build a sledding vehicle, even if it was just cardboard cut from a box from Mr. Fuller's store.

In the springtime when sap flowed in the arms and trunks of New Hampshire maples, Edwin tapped the trees. With skillful hands that would serve him well during World War II in Iran and India, he built spouts which would be driven into the tree trunks after using Dad's bitstock to drill a hole. Edwin cut a 4-inch wood branch with a soft center and hollowed it out to form a tube exactly the size of the hole in the tree.

A nail held a bucket under the spout, and we all waited. Edwin often harvested maple sap from 10 or more trees and drained two or three buckets from each. Ten-quart pails ran over with sap sometimes, and he sent us kids to check the buckets more than once each day. The grand old maple trees produced the sweetest syrup (just like the way it should be with the dispositions of grandparents and elders in a church).

Mom's multi-gallon clothes boiler held our pails of maple sap, and we placed this big container atop a firebox to bring the sap to a slow boil. Sap has a high boiling point, and it took days to render the thick liquid down to the right pancake-lovin' texture.

Scattered through our chores and projects as a family, time with boys and girls from other families peppered our lives. Often a couple boys followed me home after school, and we cleaned stalls or chopped wood. Wayne Hoyt and Roland Goddard came to be a part of the Seppala clan over the years, and I believe that Mom helped shape them into good men. She never hid her light "under a bushel."

The hymns she sang while she planted flowers carried a loving message, even when my friends didn't understand all the words. Her hope for each young man (who wolfed down her coffee cakes which Finnish folks call "nisu") was for them to repent and believe in Jesus Christ. As years passed, we all grasped what righteousness really looked like. Mom lived it out: washing clothes, picking blueberries, even when she scolded us for tracking mud into the kitchen. And we learned about God's grace when she forgave so very quickly.

෧෧෧

It was the 1930s. No Finn would have conceived that his sons would be conscripted to serve the nation that had adopted them. After the devastation of World War I, Germany was awakening with a voice promising a new era of prosperity and power. Adolf Hitler spoke of better days ahead, with Europe ripe for conquest. But many of my school friends would later fight to keep Nazi oppression away from our shores, and all of us sitting at those little desks would be enlisted in some way to defend America during the war years.

Before I knew it, I felt my childhood passing. I was now on the top floor of our Rindge school, a confident, strong eighth-grader. Miss Youngquest taught me for two years, and my abilities in math showed through all my other subjects. This teacher had a special gift few teachers today seem able to muster: She tapped my imagination and rendered it down to real life. Apples suddenly had meaning beyond their sweet taste. They represented budgeting and accounting and investing. I grew restless just sitting in hard desks ever learning, learning. I was itching to put my imagination and drive to work!

One more year, and perhaps I could start my life as a man — if I could only convince my mother.

Chapter two
Tempests and travels

My father lived only one generation away from true subsistence farming. Each morning he searched the New Hampshire skies like any man of the soil. When Dad had settled upon his course, he'd stride purposefully to the barn or his Farmall tractor, with Wally and me trying to match his pace. God has embedded an agricultural awareness into the DNA of most Finns. Hayfields and gardens, eggs and cream churn in our souls. Elders such as me gaze heavenward each day like battered weathervanes, forecasting fair or foul weather by aching knees or swelling knuckles.

I was 12 years old, a student in the upper room of Miss Youngquest's class at the Rindge school, when, right about potato harvest, the most devastating storm in half a century gyrated toward the East Coast. The "Long Island Express" slammed into our unsuspecting county on the 21st of September 1938.

Thunderheads had been drifting lazily all afternoon atop Rindge's 50-acre crown of ancient pine trees, about 500 feet east of our house. Dad and Mom had been sky watching, and we expected an autumn rainstorm.

As we finished up our chores, slate-gray clouds corrupted the bright white thunderheads above the pines, and shadow smothered our valley. The ominous presence boiled out of the southeast from Rhode Island, and suddenly a vanguard of rain signaled that something had been unleashed. A torrent of showers drenched down upon tin and shingles, filling swales in the yard and chasing chickens under cars and porches.

Mom and Dad, Arthur, Edwin, Wallace, Alvina, Evelyn,

The best is yet to come

Edna, Elaine and I ambled about, snug inside our living room and kitchen. It felt a little like a holiday at first, all of us together, laughing as we nibbled Finnish *pulla*, a sweet coffee bread. But then the curtains started moving with the doors shut tight. Wind and water washed under the threshold, and everyone stared, as though we expected someone to burst through the door. Even little Elaine grew quiet and clung to Mom's neck.

The electric lights flickered, then after one boisterous gust, they went out, the girls gasping in the dusky haze. Dad and Arthur dug out candles and lanterns, and Mom found matches in the kitchen drawer for lighting wicks. Eerie shadows danced to a frightening overture, seeming to celebrate the riot outside. We measured the wind's intensity by the sounds of "shrapnel" clattering against the house — the size of hens' eggs, then of whole chickens!

"Gettin' stronger," Dad said as he rose from his chair. He strode to the south wall and placed a big hand against the cool windowpane, feeling the vibration.

"Sounds like a train's gonna run over us," I said, and everyone glanced at Dad nervously.

"Is it a nor'easter, Dad?" Arthur asked.

"Could very well be." He found my mother's eyes. "But I never have seen one *this* bad."

In fact, few in Cheshire County had, especially immigrant Finns. The last major hurricane had ripped the East Coast in 1869, and that "circular storm" (as they were called then) made landfall in Southern Maine. It had shredded the coastline as far as the Canadian Outer Banks. More than 100 people had lost their lives.

While we prayed for the winds to die down in Rindge, New Hampshire, gusts in neighboring Massachusetts were reaching 186 miles per hour. New York's Empire State Building swayed drunkenly, and 13 feet of water flooded downtown Providence,

Tempests and travels

Rhode Island. Massive tides sucked whole communities out to sea, and residents survived by clinging to debris, some swept as far south as Connecticut.

In the house my father built, we huddled together like rabbits in a burrow, listening to the deafening howl outside. In the worst gusts, we watched windowpanes billow inward toward us like pillowcases on Mom's clothesline. At these times Dad would hop up and gently press against the pane to keep it from shattering. All four of us boys imitated him at different windows as he hollered, "Don't push too hard, now!"

No one slept, not even dozed off. About midnight, a roaring gust plucked up our chicken coop and rolled it toward us. The hurricane dashed the whole building against the corner of our house, and we instinctively assembled away from the crashing sounds, across the room.

"Are we blowing away?" Alvina cried, and Dad shone a lantern outside through a window where parts of the twisted henhouse flapped and groaned.

"No, no. But the chickens will need a new place to lay their eggs!"

Dad was laughing aloud, but his voice sounded strained. Our coop was just one of the many buildings that would need repair or replacing all over Cheshire County. Daylight would tell the tale.

"How far you think the coop flew?" Arthur asked, shaking his head.

"Got to be at least 140, maybe 150 feet," Edwin said, chuckling along with Dad. My father kept a brave face for our sakes. And no one felt jolly enough to quip that the chicken coop and our house were probably built by the same Finn carpenters.

The eye of the storm passed over, and in the "respite" of several minutes, Dad walked outside and shined a little light on damages before the wind reclaimed intensity and blew from the other direction. The back of the storm lasted for several more hours, and it sometimes sounded as if cows or horses were being slammed against the house.

Miraculously, we all escaped harm, and not a pane of glass even cracked. The first Seppala to ever step ashore at New York City could not have gaped with more wonder than we did as morning broke, and we stared at the landscape outside our front door.

Rindge had been sheared and stomped by mighty drunken giants. Maples and elms, my old climbing pals, leaned on their sides, split and beaten. Telephone poles by the dozens looked like oversized toothpicks flung from great heights and jammed into the earth. Black electric wires snaked through ditches and around trees. All was deathly silent in a bright blue, sunny *gloom.*

All along Payson Hill Road, the hurricane relocated any barn or outbuilding not anchored to earth or bolted to a foundation. No vehicle, two-wheel or four, powered by motor or horse, traveled that road, nor could they. Debris of all sizes and shapes spoiled the thoroughfare.

"Oh, God!"

With a cupped hand, my father shaded his weary eyes from the sun, gazing toward Rindge's ancient pine forest. He trotted forward, and I tripped along in his muddy wake, shivering against the morning breeze.

All the vertical green and gray pillars were gone. In their place, muddy earth and gnarled witch's fingers tangled at the base of hundreds of prostrate pines. The high canopy of needles that had whispered comfort to us on so many picnics covered the earth like a tattered green shroud, as if trying to hide its disfigured limbs. No slip of a whittling knife had ever wounded me as badly as feeling Dad's loss that September day, as he stared at the grove.

Shouts and the sounds of creaking machinery woke me the

Tempests and travels

next morning. At daybreak, Dad, Edwin and Arthur were already on the street with a dozen men or more, sawing downed trees blocking the Payson Hill Road. The county hired men to clear roads and repair buildings, and boys of 16 years or more made out like bandits. I growled like a caged fox, checking off a list of cleanup chores that Mom assigned me, while my brothers and other boys raked in the dough.

As a 12 year old, my mind barely comprehended the damage around Rindge, much less the devastation of an entire region. As I groused about my age and chores, thousands along the East Coast wept over their losses. More than 600 people died in the hurricane that sailors called The Yankee Clipper.

Our pine forest was just a fraction of an estimated two billion trees felled by the storm. No one ever replanted the trees, and 50 years later, I could still see pine stumps where I napped on a carpet of soft needles. In fact, all of New England seemed to have aged overnight, forever traumatized by this one horrific September night.

Months after the hurricane, government-paid loggers descended upon our prone forest to salvage the lumber before carpenter ants and rot turned the wood to sawdust. Tractors dragged hundreds of the denuded trunks to a staging area where logs were separated into lumber types. Log trucks then hauled them to Crow Croft Pond, along the road to Fitchburg. In the water, these "soaked" logs were preserved for years. A man could walk across the pond atop these floating tree trunks.

The remaining logs they threw into Pearly Lake, on the road to Keene. Pearly was just that, our pristine "pearl" — as clear a lake as a family could savor for a summer swim. However, the dead pines shocked the lake so badly that the water changed to a color of decomposing brown bark and remains so to this day.

For months, two hives of portable sawmills buzzed early and late on the banks of these lakes, salvaging millions of board

The best is yet to come

feet of lumber. Many a carpenter on the East Coast hammered a stick or two of our pine forest in house or barn for years to come.

Even as the Long Island Express invaded the East Coast, a global political storm brewed across the sea a continent away. In Europe, Adolf Hitler wearied of playing one nation against another, and in 1939, his Nazis invaded Poland, triggering the bloody Second World War. Three months later, Joseph Stalin beefed up Russian borders in fear of Nazi aggression, and like the former Czars of Russia, he set his jaw to steal Finland's sovereignty. With a vast array of planes, tanks and troops, the Soviet Union trampled Finn villages to subjugate my father's homeland.

ॐॐॐ

The visiting Finnish pastor stopped preaching and glared at us. "If you boys don't stop horsing around up there, I tell you, I'm going to preach all night!"

From the church balcony, Wally and I glanced down at Dad's face, frown furrows deepening above his dark brows. Mom's brown eyes got *big* when she was steamed.

She signaled us with one finger, and we scurried like squirrels down the stairs and into the pew beside her, thoroughly chastened. Our church on Poor Farm Road in New Ipswich swelled with nearly 100 children, and their family names were as familiar to me as Mom's dinner plates: Aho, Antilla, Kangas, Granfors, Gedenberg and Somero.

Services were conducted mostly in Finnish, but times were changing. Children of immigrants were creating a culture distinctly "Finnish American." There was talk of providing English language services, along with Finnish. Not all of the younger people understood Finnish as well as the older folks anymore.

Tempests and travels

Anytime visiting pastors from the homeland held special services, they carried the gospel, plus news about the tank battles and skirmishes raging in the villages where our grandmas had planted gardens and grandpas had chopped wood. Many pastors in Finland doubled as soldiers and fought with their flocks against Soviet invaders. We listened to radio broadcasts about the battles in a brutally cold Scandinavian winter; at times it seemed hopeless to push back against the might of Soviet Russia.

Home after Sunday services, every subject from war to church business came up for discussion at the Seppala table. And lately our church had some real interesting business.

We were finishing up bucket-sized bowls of *loxlotta* (a scalloped potato fish casserole) when Edwin asked, "Do you think they'll sell?"

He passed a pitcher of milk to Dad. It was fresh from the cow that Sunday morning.

"Looks like it. We might be carrying pews down the street to the Baptist Church next week."

"Will we change the name to Apostolic Lutheran?" Wally asked.

"Course we will, silly," Arthur said with a mouthful of potatoes.

We were all watching Mom as she flopped a long sweet loaf of *pulla* onto a towel at the counter. She crowned it with butter churned by Edna and Evelyn, and we scraped our plates clean a little faster. Mom sat down, glancing around at the dishes and grins.

So glad we're all here and not in Finland, Lord.

If they were in Finland, all of her boys and Gus, too, would be fighting the Red Army, along with her father and brothers. Nothing would keep her men from taking up arms to defend their families on their own soil.

That evening we crowded around the radio to hear the

The best is yet to come

latest about the Finnish Winter War and about the occupation of Poland. Nazis had committed mass murder in Western Poland, and Mom felt ill when her sons talked about joining the Army.

If this madman, Hitler, continues his march across Europe, how can a mother keep her sons away from war?

At least they wouldn't take Martin, because of his bad eye. She never thought she would bless that drunken doctor. But she did that night.

෯෯෯

The Baptist congregation had dwindled to three elderly women, and indeed, they were willing to sell their building, especially when they heard the buyers were believers in Jesus, too. Mom loved the clock in the steeple tower, and with a basement, a large sanctuary and a roomy balcony upstairs, the Baptist church building had plenty of room for more — children!

The next week the decision was made to purchase the Baptist church, situated right in the center of New Ipswich. A buyer had already stepped up to buy the old Apostolic Lutheran Church building: Matti Somero. When he handed over the asking price of $50, everyone wondered just what Matti planned to do with his own church.

Four Apostolic Lutheran men trouped off to pay three Baptist ladies for their church. They greeted the Finns with decorum and grace. After the polite small talk, our representatives handed over the agreed-upon price of $200, but the Baptists suddenly smiled and shook their heads.

"I'm sorry, but $200 is quite difficult to divide between the three of us. Could you please just give us $50 each, to make it easier for us?"

Our thrifty Finns happily agreed.

Tempests and travels

The first Sunday at the spacious New Ipswich Apostolic Lutheran Church was a time of celebration for God's bounty and blessing. The three Baptist women attended that day and thereafter quite regularly, though they did not know a word of Finnish. I always wondered what they thought of our services, almost always the same in form. First, we all sang a hymn. Then Pastor Emanuel Aho would lead in prayer. Another song, and then our pastor read scripture relating to the sermon. Next came a sermon that, hopefully, ultimately led a seeking person to repentance and service to Jesus Christ.

The Baptist ladies always said that they felt the Holy Spirit when they came to our church.

As for Matti: He disassembled the old church, piece by piece, and hauled it to his farm to build the most "sanctified" barn in Hillsborough County.

ॐॐॐ

"Cut him down the center, and peel back the skin, quills and all."

I watched, wincing a little, as my Boy Scout leader, Russell White, slit the porcupine's belly. About six of us 14 year olds had run the creature to ground, then stared as Mr. White clubbed him twice, until the animal lay quivering on the ground.

"Martin, gather some wood. Roland, you build the fire. We're gonna have some fried porgypine!"

My best pal, Roland Goddard, had convinced me to join the Scouts, and it was a blast! A couple other local boys, Wayne Holt and Reginald Davis, had joined about the same time as I had, and now we sat around the crackling fire, nibbling porcupine on a stick. The wild greasy meat went down hard, while Mr. Russell, leaning against his backpack and chewing contentedly, instructed us.

The best is yet to come

"Always be prepared, boys. That's the Scout motto. Carry a knife wherever you go, and in the woods take matches with you — you might need to spend a night if an emergency comes up. And what's the slowest game in the woods?"

"Porgypine!" we all shouted, raising whittled sticks into the air like musketeers.

"Right. He's survival food. What's our Scout creed?"

"A Scout is always trustworthy, loyal, helpful, cheerful, kind, thrifty, brave, clean and reverent!" we repeated together. I never forgot the "bark-like" taste of porgypine or the Scout creed.

At Rindge, moral men and women helped train young people to take the reins of the community later in life. Basic Biblical values were harnessed to lifestyles, then passed on to the next generation. Families watched for ways to help boys excel and gain confidence, not just through lecturing, but by cultivating experiences and relationships.

I was 14 when I took on my first building project for a "customer": Pastor Fletcher, from the Congregational Church. One day he hallooed me for a chat as I trotted past his house in coveralls.

"Martin, you think you could build me a chicken coop?"

I hesitated a full blink, trying to stifle a grin before I answered, "Yes, sir."

Mr. Fletcher waved a hand toward a dilapidated shed. "You can get all your boards from there. When can you start?"

Dad cut me loose from a few summer chores, so I got right to work yanking out nails, tearing out 2x4s and siding and separating them. Dad trusted me with his precious carpenter tools, adding a boost to my confidence. I drew up a common-sense plan in my head, then started building. A door and window adorned the coop, and after the feathered occupants "approved" their new home, the pastor paid me.

I had completed my first job as a contractor! I never forgot

Tempests and travels

the lesson of falling back upon common sense when considering untried designs. That first building served as a triumphal arch that I marched through to tackle multi-million-dollar projects all over the East Coast.

It all started with a preacher's chicken coop.

કર્ટ કર્ટ કર્ટ

I loved the attic of Uncle Bill's cottage in New Ipswich. Roland Goddard and I bunked there on and off for the three months of apple-picking season.

The orchard provided pickers with 10-foot-long stepladders and buckets with canvas bottoms that dropped open by a lever. I strapped the bucket around my neck and picked apples hour upon hour, as steady as the engine in Dad's Farmall.

After picking from the ground, rung by rung, I'd climb the ladder to strip every higher limb. With a brimming bucket, I then straddled a wood bushel box and flipped the bucket lever, opening the canvas bottom and dropping the apples into the box. Each box held two apple buckets, and every full box of apples was 10 cents in my hand. In about eight hours I filled 110 bushels, earning 11 bucks!

The average hourly wage in the early 1940s was about 75 cents per hour, so we boys rolled in tall clover. Martin Somero was about as fast a picker as me, and we would race like calves to the feedlot, filling boxes of beautiful McIntosh, Cortland, Baldwin and Northern Spy apples for pies that cooled on windowsills all over Cheshire County. This experience with "piece work" trained me to always give incentives for men in my employ.

While we were picking apples in September 1940, Franklin Roosevelt signed into law the first peacetime draft in American history. Sixteen million men would register for the armed services.

The best is yet to come

In Paris, Adolf Hitler surveyed his newly acquired treasures. After invading France, his bombs fell on London, and by the end of the year, Italy and Japan had signed a pact with Germany to establish a "new order" in the world.

In the bitter winter of 1940, the battle of Suomussalmi helped resolve the Winter War in Finland. Joseph Stalin lost nearly 55,000 troops in one grand blundered attempt to control Finland militarily. Finnish freedom fighters on skis savaged the Russian and Ukrainian soldiers on and off the Finnish thoroughfares. Deep snows bogged down tanks, and the Soviets still alive abandoned their artillery and supplies to the Finns. After a few more months of unsuccessful incursions, Stalin offered conditions of peace. In a Soviet Union-Finland treaty, the Finnish leaders accepted harsh terms to end the bloodshed, and Finland has never been free of communist influence since.

During that same year, I came down with a severe sore throat and high fever.

Mom and Dad rushed me to see Dr. Emerson. I sat weakly in his exam room where I heard a phrase I would hear over and over the following weeks whenever the doctor visited our house: "Open wide, son."

My throat was coated with angry red welts, and my tongue was as red as strawberries. My chest and armpits looked almost sunburned, and he stuck a thermometer in my mouth while he talked to Mom.

"I believe the boy's got scarlet fever, Annie."

Mom was quiet, and Dad put an arm around her. Pain in my throat had been growing worse for two days before they drove me in to see the doc.

"Hmmm, 103 degrees. Better get him to bed. And the house needs to be quarantined, Gus. Choose who'll be caring for him, and keep him isolated. Someone from the city'll be out and put a quarantine notice on your door."

We rode home in silence, me leaning on Mom's shoulder,

the shock of Dr. Emerson's dire words sinking in slowly. As soon as we arrived home, Dad walled off a bedroom for me and warned everyone to keep out. Mom would be my nurse for nearly six weeks.

Extending from ground to window over the long porch in front of our house, Dad leaned a tall ladder to connect the upper bedrooms to the outside world. As I lay there, burning up, I could hear my brothers and sisters ascending and descending.

Mom suffered right along with me before my fever dropped to normal levels. Raging night and day, the back of my throat and mouth throbbed like fire ants coated every inch. My joints ached, and at times I fell into a delirium that frightened Mom to tears.

"Dad! Why is that tractor moving ahead! The wheels aren't even turning!"

All she could do was calm me with gentle words, stroking my brow with cool fingers. I knew she was crying, but I couldn't keep track of things coming out of my mouth. For 10 painful days, Mom prayed me through the worst of my scarlet fever.

Chicken soup. Beef soup. Potato soup. I gained strength little by little, but Mom's chunky Martin was gone. My only consolation after being isolated for six long weeks: Edwin told me that I had grown taller.

One day toward the end of my quarantine, when I was strong enough to sit up in bed, Mom came in looking serious. "Marty, if God had called you home in this sickness, do you feel that you would have been ready to go?"

Tears welled up in my eyes, and I held my peace, as I often did when confronted about spiritual things. I felt that God had shined a searchlight on my soul. I wanted to make something of myself right here on earth, but the Holy Spirit was speaking to me about my eternal destiny.

The last time Dr. Emerson dropped by the house to check

on my progress, my bantam-weight physician met me shoveling dirt in the garden. He reached out a hand to me, and I grabbed his. I could tell he was pleased about my strong recovery.

"Good honest dirt, son," he said, rubbing his hand on a black trouser leg.

Sometimes at church, when one of our lay preachers taught from the word of God, I had to hide my eyes for fear the kids might call me crybaby. After my bout with scarlet fever, I grew more and more responsive to Jesus' voice in my life.

One Sunday we visited the Litchfield church where I sat with a bunch of my pals: Leo, Leonard, Martin, Phillip, Wallace, Ervin, William, Bob (all Someros), as well as Bill Hjalmer and Dick Aho. We listened from the balcony as usual as Pastor John Paana talked about God's mercy.

Suddenly I felt *burdened*, like a Boy Scout with a backpack full of rocks. I yearned to *know* that I would go to heaven when I died, but I choked back my tears and didn't speak about it.

About a year later, when Pastor Arnold Anderson held services at our New Ipswich church, I finally emptied that pack once and for all. I recall that Mom and Dad were at this special service. I sat close to the pulpit, on the right-hand side, and I guess the Spirit of God decided it was time to pour the foundation for my faith. I might as well have been trying to hold back the Nashua River, my tears flowed so freely, and Pastor Arnold sat down beside me after the service.

"What's wrong, son? Can I help you? Do you have sin to confess?"

I nodded yes, and he smiled and put a strong hand on my shoulder. "Do you believe that Jesus' precious blood is the payment for your sins?"

"Yes, sir," I answered, sniffing.

"Do you believe that all your sins are forgiven, in the name and by the precious reconciling blood of Jesus?"

I swiped at my nose and nodded. He invited my mother to

join us, and as soon as she sat beside me, I felt a fresh gully-washer coming on. "Oh, Mom …" A wave of gratitude for her love and care swept over me, and I pulled out all the things I had ever done that might have hurt her, confessing them aloud.

"Marty, you know I forgive you. And I say that you are forgiven in Jesus' name and by the power of his blood."

I cannot describe the mysterious relief that rose from my soul. The "pack" was *empty*, except for the essential assurance that I was clean and forgiven. I knew that I was a child of God and that heaven was my true home.

Searching my heart these many years later, I believe that God's grace covered me from an early age. I have always believed that Jesus was my Savior. But while sitting in that hardwood pew with my mother that evening, God strengthened my faith to know I was saved. I have been comforted by this experience my whole life, and since that time, I have carried in my "pack" only the essentials that Jesus gives me to bear.

ॐॐॐ

After graduating eighth grade from my Rindge school, I enrolled at Conant High School in Jaffrey, where I excelled in my favorite subject: math. I was 15 years old and full of a youthful impatience that I struggled to throttle back. I sensed that my destiny lay among working men and machinery, so I mapped out a course to quit school and get a job when I turned16. I studied hard until then, chomping at the bit to finish up ninth grade.

I made the honor roll at Conant, and my brother Wally (he stayed back one grade and graduated from Rindge with me) and friends Wayne Hoyt and Roland Goddard attended most of the same classes. We caught a ride to school in Jaffrey each day, because, like balls and bats, our town provided nothing except the "basics" for our education.

The best is yet to come

My first experience designing a project from schematics took shape in Manual Training class at Conant, the one course that truly held my interest. I asked my teacher if I had permission to engineer a practical device for my mom, one that I had seen somewhere.

"Go ahead, Marty, but I don't think you have the skills to create such a thing. Give it a try, though, and I'll give you a hand."

I drew up my schematic the way I saw Dad sketch out plans for his projects, all the while cogitating about Mom's time-consuming process: washing, drying and ironing curtains. If my plan worked, Mom could skip ironing altogether. Her curtains would dry stiff as a board on a "stretcher" that accommodated various-sized curtains.

I finished the working model of a curtain stretcher during the school year. My teacher liked my curtain stretcher so much that he asked for schematics so he could build a stretcher for his wife. Mom loved my creation, and I hoped she wouldn't balk at my plan when I told her I was done with school.

After school and on weekends, I made forays into Jaffrey, exploring job prospects. I marched out of Conant armed with youth and ambition, and my hopes for landing a job fell into place like pins in a trailer hitch. Mom and Dad discussed my plans and set down the same rules for me as they had for Edwin and Arthur when they quit school: $5 per week for board and help with chores as long as I lived at home.

I applied for work at the Winchendon Mill, a textile plant that manufactured denim cloth from cotton. The personnel manager looked me over with a cautious eye. He told me to come back when I was 16. He would give me a job with starting pay of 37 ½ cents per hour, if I could handle the work.

"Here's what the job entails, son. You'll be tracking every bolt of cloth that comes off the line and keeping accounts of yardage on each bolt. Then you'll add the yards and keep account of the total that goes into each bale. These bales weigh 500 pounds each. Think you can do it?"

"Yes, sir!"

"Then see you in a month or so."

It was hard enough getting back and forth to school, but now I had to think about how I was going to get to work. So my next obstacle was buying a car.

"Hey, Arthur. Can you lend me a few bucks for a car? I got a job now in Jaffrey, so I can pay you back right away."

Arthur gave me the money gladly. We Seppala boys all bought cars as soon as we turned 16: It was our induction into a hard-charging work ethic that stuck with us for a lifetime.

Arthur drove me to see a 1937 Ford, and I gave the man $150 after a test drive. I took my driver's test in Jaffrey and passed it on my birthday. The testing officer knew I had been driving for some time, so smoothly did I shift the gears. Now I had spankin' new license plates on the '37 and a card that said I was legal to tear all over Cheshire County.

I never expected to find a lasting friendship at the Winchendon Mill. A young man named Roland Sharp lived close by and ate lunch at home each day. As we got to know each other, he asked me to come home and eat with him and his family. Seldom did I have to bring a lunch with me to work. I immediately returned the favor, and Roland came home to meet my family.

Sometimes I worried that friends who met my "preacher" mother might be put off by her very personal and direct approach in discussing their spiritual condition. But looking back, I recall that people of many cultures and backgrounds visited our home and seldom just one time. While speaking to Roland, Mom discovered that thundershowers terrified him and his mother to such a degree that they would cringe behind locked doors with rosary beads, petitioning Mary for protection until the storm passed.

The best is yet to come

One Saturday Roland brought his mother, father and uncle to use our sauna, a unique experience for many who visited us Seppalas. Roland's uncle took the first bath, closing the door with a big grin. Roland's folks sat at our kitchen table and talked with us until we heard heavy breathing in the front room.

There stood Roland's uncle, beet-red, sweating and shaky. Dad went to the sauna and noticed that soap suds floated inside our 55-gallon barrel of hot water, and the lid was off. Uncle said that he had dumped some cool water from a rinsing pail into the barrel of boiling water, then soaped up and jumped in! He looked like a boiled lobster, and all Mom could think of to help was to offer Uncle a cool glass of well water. We men kept our laughter harnessed fairly well until our new friends left.

I worked at Winchendon for several months, but my friendship with Roland and his family lasted for years. My next job, working for George Todd and the town of Rindge, taught me not to "count my chickens before they hatched."

I loved horse trading and swapped my '37 Ford for a dump truck (remember, I'm 16 years old here), thinking that I could hire out hauling gravel for the city. After my steady work each day, I sometimes hauled junk for farmers, but it didn't pay much. I had this great scheme to make the truck pay for itself. Mr. Todd had agreed to hire me, but then backtracked.

"I'm sorry, Marty, but I've got men with families who need the work more than you do."

So there I was, stuck with a big ol' dump truck that broke down regularly and guzzled fuel like a plow horse in a grain silo! I drove it around town like a passenger car, taking up three car lengths wherever I parked it. After I sold it, I was glad to see the old truck parked at someone else's farm.

Mr. Todd had three NETCO trucks for winter plowing, and the first thing I did when he offered to hire me as a driver was bury one in a snowdrift — with him sitting beside me. I hit a drift like a bull ramming a steel girder, and the snow berm sucked me right into the ditch. It took Mr. Todd, me and another worker, Tommy Pentila, quite a while to dig out the heavy rig.

Back on the icy road, Mr. Todd looked a little red in the face. "Marty," he said, "please, don't do that again. It's cold out there!"

When I was 17, our nation found itself fighting two enemies of freedom: Germany in Europe and Japan in the Pacific Islands. Farm boys waved draft letters while their mothers cried, and radios blared of desperate battles at Bataan, Philippines and Guadalcanal. Hitler's war machine rolled to Stalingrad, USSR, and Rindge felt the icy touch of war in its drives to collect metals and in sudden gasoline rationing.

Edwin had been gone for months, training in the Army Air Corps after being called up to serve. At 17, my bullheaded resolve to join the Army Air Corps finally met the granite-hard stubbornness of my Finnish mother.

To find a path to the armed services, I enlisted friends in my quest, like Harris Rice, who owned the blueberry field we rented. A general in the Army Air Corps was his personal friend, and I was excited when he told me that he could get me in, even if I was legally blind in my one eye. I headed home, rehearsing how I would tell Mom about my good fortune.

In the meantime, Mr. Harris called my mother to discuss her son's future.

"Martin will need a parent's signature to join, Mrs. Seppala. Will you sign?"

"Never, Mr. Harris, and I *mean* it! I have given one son to the war already."

I tried to join the Merchant Marines when I was 18, but they detected a heart murmur during my exam. Could a heart condition have developed when I had scarlet fever? For his own reasons, God did not want me to serve in jungles, in airplane hangars or on the high seas. I can accept it now. But as a young man, I questioned his purposes. I finally received a "limited service" letter, but never heard from the U.S. Government again.

❧ ❧ ❧

I believe the Holy Spirit orchestrated well-ordered awakenings in my early life during three journeys I made: one while I was in grade school, the other two during my teens.

My father was known to keep his roomy 1930 four-door Essex in tiptop shape. So our Apostolic Lutheran congregation asked him to bring home some Finn preachers landing at the New York harbor. These men were planning to tour the denomination's churches from New Hampshire to California. Uncle Bill would accompany Dad, and I barely contained my joy when my father asked me if I wanted to go, too. I packed for a three-day odyssey, and Miss Conner, my teacher, gave me permission to miss school if I would give a report about the whole trip to our lower floor of students, grades one to six.

After driving our Essex 250 miles to the "Big Apple," Dad rented a hotel room in a building several stories high. My big grin during my first elevator ride spread to everyone inside the car watching me. It was like a horse stall that floated up and down!

The vastness of New York City in 1934 startled me with its human throngs and buildings reaching higher than the tallest trees of Rindge. Massive skyscrapers rivaling Mount Monadnock in height and breadth crowded the skyline, seemingly without end. And the knowledge that each building had been conceived in a man's mind, charted on paper and constructed in steel birthed an excitement in me that just grew and grew.

Lights! I could see them as far as my eye could focus, twinkling like stars and representing the busy lives of millions of people. Uncle Bill snored in his bed, while my father and I marveled at the city as we looked out from several stories high. I couldn't wait to see what was on the menu for breakfast.

After flapjacks in a restaurant near the hotel lobby, Dad drove us to the docks where an elongated hotel, as long as three of Mr. Harris' blueberry fields, floated on the water: Dad said it was a ship! Hundreds of passengers waved colorful kerchiefs from the railing, while others disembarked over wide gangplanks reaching to the pier. Massive containers on cranes were hoisted and swung back and forth like my rope swing back home, and Dad chatted with uniformed men who could help us locate our Finn visitors. Their ship was called the SS *Bremen*, the most advanced German high-speed steam turbine ocean liner of her day.

I stuck close to Dad and Uncle Bill, a little worried that I might be swept away in the swarms of people on the pier. After several hours waiting, we shook hands with three Finnish men: Analli and Jamsa, the preachers, and Kasu, a man of stature and wealth in Finland.

Dad tied down their luggage to the top of the Essex, and we piled in, rain pelting the windshield, wipers flapping and excited Finnish spreading as thick as butter inside. I was an exhausted little gypsy by the time we reached a restaurant, and I slept through the whole meal and conversations. Mr. Kasu said it was his treat, and to this day, I regret sleeping through a dinner of *anything* I could have chosen on the menu!

Back home, how could I possibly articulate the immensity of New York or my awakening to limitless possibilities in my future? As a third-grader, I did my best, and Miss Conner gave me an A for my presentation.

My consciousness to bigotry was awakened on a trip south when I was 16. I had been working at Winchendon Mill when my brother Edwin called to invite us to his graduation from Emery Riddle School of Aviation at Miami Beach, Florida. His

The best is yet to come

class of 1942 would sail to Persia soon, but he hoped to visit home once before he shipped out. Dad and especially Mom couldn't wait to see their son after so many months away from the farm. At the time, my hopes to follow in my brother's aviation footsteps soared. I quit my job to see him graduate.

My father and mother couldn't leave the farm, but Arthur, my good friend Roland Sharp and I boarded a crowded Greyhound Bus at Fitchburg, Massachusetts, heading to Miami Beach to see Edwin receive his awards.

My first bus ride opened my eyes to mass transportation and the corrupt pecking order that survived long after the war over slavery ended. We took a bus to New York City, then on to Richmond, Virginia, where a crowd milled about waiting to board. Night and day these Greyhounds ran, but at Richmond, the passengers seemed split into two groups, like some unseen hand forced them to keep separate. One group seemed to hold power over the other.

Blacks used separate restrooms and eateries and were shooed away from the nicer "Whites Only" areas, like stray cats from a porch. Black people stood together, watching as our bus arrived, and an attendant in a rumpled uniform and sweaty cap dropped a rope to let a couple families through. They knew exactly where to go: *the back of the bus*. The rest of the black folk in line were shunted to the side to make way for us white folk to fill up the remaining seats.

As our Greyhound roared out of the terminal, dozens of dark faces watched me, expressionless, and my gut felt queasy, like I had witnessed an assault, helpless to intervene. It was my first encounter with stark, ugly segregation.

We arrived in Jacksonville, Florida, and the air in the bus seemed breathable again when passengers of every color mingled in the seats. Sweat soaked our clothes when we finally got off at the Miami Beach terminal. Then we New England boys found that the hotel Edwin had reserved for the three of us had no air conditioning, except a breeze from an open window.

Roland had warned us briefly about his occasional epileptic seizures, but I was unprepared for the experience. His uncontrollable movements and sounds made the hairs on my neck prickle, and I prayed the seizure would pass quickly. In just a few months I would understand the helplessness a "handicapped" person feels at times when *I* was rejected from serving my country in the military. Roland took his lifetime ordeal in stride, and I had to learn to do the same.

Edwin treated us to a big meal after his graduation, and we bid him farewell, expecting him home on furlough before he left overseas. But my brother shipped out the next week. Mom cried and cried over not seeing him before he went to war.

"I'm of a mind to write President Roosevelt about this! It's so unfair. What if I never see him again?" She never wrote the Commander in Chief, and Edwin ended up in Burma, patching up planes for the Flying Tigers after dogfights with Japanese Zeros.

But we never saw Edwin until after World War II ended.

The third excursion that struck my heart happened when I was 17 years old. I drove to North Hampton, Massachusetts, to see my uncle Wally, who was dying of tuberculosis.

My father's brother was as unlike my uncle Bill as vinegar and honey. Both men were bachelors all their lives, and our family cherished them equally. But Bill brightened our lives with God's love whenever he came to visit. Wally worried us.

Whenever he stayed with us, often weeks at a time, he made up the same excuse for one of us to take him to town on Saturday morning.

"Marty, can I get a lift to Winchendon? My watch isn't running right, and I need a jeweler to look it over …"

In Winchendon, he'd point at the jeweler's and say, "Drop me there, and I'll find a ride home." A block away, his friends bellied up to a bar in a local tavern, and I knew that's where he ended up. Uncle Wally was a weekend alcoholic. If the door was locked when he stumbled back to our house, he'd sleep in the barn.

One morning, after sleeping near the cows, he came into the house with manure on his clothes, which didn't set well with Mom. Knowing my mother, I'm sure he heard many times about his need to repent and that Jesus loved him.

One cold winter, on a drunken binge, my uncle fell into a snowy gutter, and no one found him for hours. Pneumonia set in while he was in the hospital, and he contracted tuberculosis.

After a long drive to North Hampton, I climbed the steps of the hospital considering what I should say to this man I had known my whole life. At the front desk, I asked about him. The nurse just shook her head. "Mr. Seppala has advanced TB of the bone. He's not long for this earth, I'm afraid." She pointed me to his room.

"Marty! Good to see you!" My uncle looked frail, unshaven and his voice was weak.

After a little small talk, I got down to business, gently telling him that Jesus loved him, would forgive him and would prepare a place for him in heaven.

He held up a shaky hand and shut my words out with quivering, closed eyelids.

"Martin, I know that you would like to have many people come to your church ..."

Uncle Wally thought I was recruiting him to fill a pew! He confused church attendance with a personal relationship with Jesus, and I felt like I had failed my mission as I drove home to Rindge.

Wally lived a few months longer. My brother Arthur made the trip to North Hampton, too, to share the gospel with him one last time. But our uncle simply refused to yield to God's Spirit, even knowing that he had a short time to live. He died with a hard, unbelieving heart.

Tempests and travels

My journey to see Uncle Wally struck a sad and lasting note in my soul, but shaped my attitude over these many years regarding others who stand close to eternity. I am hopeful for them to repent and receive eternal life through the precious blood of our Savior, *but it is their choice.*

I can only pray that God's grace breaks through their unbelief before it's too late.

Chapter three
Forming foundations

During the Second World War, Germany demanded that the Finnish government deport hundreds of its Jewish refugees to become part of Hitler's "Final Solution" (the mass murder of Jews from 1941-1945).

Finland gave Germany *eight.*

The German Gestapo branded these eight refugees "saboteurs, spies and robbers" and shipped them to Auschwitz-Birkenau, a Nazi concentration and extermination camp. Finnish Lutheran pastors and their flocks were outraged at this violation of basic human rights. They believed that the Jewish people commanded a unique position in history, traced to a divine Biblical covenant. However, it was not until the year 2000 that the Finnish government (Minister Paavo Lipponen) issued an official apology to the Jewish people for Finland's restrained (but deadly) response to the Nazi summons.

The Finns fought for their survival as a democracy during World War II. To blockade the cruel imperialism of the USSR, Finland allowed Germany to stage an invasion from their soil. In this strained-but-strategic alliance, Germany dared not punish the deeply religious Finns over their refusal to enthusiastically participate in the Jewish extermination. The Finnish military also refused to be dominated by a German command, even though Finns fought alongside the Nazis against the Soviets at the border.

Finnish Jews battled side-by-side with Germans against the Soviets, and synagogues were erected for worship near battle lines. An unheard-of German-Jewish cooperation existed in this Continuation War against Stalin.

Forming foundations

Apostolic Lutheran ministers from our grandparents' homeland curtailed travel abroad during the war years, and Finnish families crowded around radios or shared letters from relatives to gather news.

My physical limitations shot down any hope of shouldering an M-1 rifle, but I charged into every civilian job I could as though I were storming a bunker. I hustled behind a road grader and unjammed rocks from its gears as if it was my life's ambition. I shoveled gravel harder and faster than my peers.

George Todd, supervisor of Rindge city maintenance, wielded my youth and vigor like a prod in the flanks of his other employees, laughing: "Why don't you guys shovel like Maarden!"

Mr. Todd sometimes swung by the house about dawn, before my feet hit the cold wood floor, honking outside my bedroom window. As I rushed through the kitchen, Mom would hand me a glass of eggs, honey and milk (my eggnog breakfast). Then I'd bound off the steps to his truck that belched exhaust into the crisp morning air. Mr. Todd knew that all he had to do was point me at a job and it was done.

I demanded much of myself. I thought that God exacted perfection from all my actions. In reality, I struggled under his gentle cultivation process: I had many seasons ahead to learn what Jesus truly expects of a man.

In one of these "seasons" with Mr. Todd's road crew, I stepped out of a rut so grooved into my soul from hearing God's servants teaching and preaching that my "sin" made me feel like a truckload of rock sat on my shoulders.

"Anyone want a beer?"

It was the same call every day before a man trotted off to buy a few brews at break time. I had always shaken my head and searched my lunchbox distractedly when someone asked, but today I heard myself say, "Bring me one, too."

When our gofer passed out the bottles, I felt obligated to

drink with the men. I'll never forget the sour taste of conviction pouring down my throat. The rest of the day, I wrestled with my weakness, and as soon as I could, I found an elder and confessed about yielding to temptation. He blessed me with forgiveness in Jesus' name and blood.

"God loves a tender conscience, Martin," he said. I never forgot the lesson: If I had been outspoken about my Christian faith at my first toss of gravel, I would have been more likely to hold fast my "testimony" to the end.

I was 17 when I trouped into Winchendon to work as a painter at Alaska Freezer. There they made wooden ice cream containers. Unpainted tubs filled the warehouse, and I worked alone, painting as many as I could in a day — the more I finished, the more money I made. Soon I graduated to my own paint booth where I sprayed steel tubs with white enamel. But by the end of the day I had breathed in so much paint, the enamel layered my nostrils and sinuses. I asked for another job in the warehouse, didn't get it and ended up leaving.

Apple picking at Heald Orchards sure was healthier, but then my friend Bob Speckman told me about a job that paid better than union wages. For a 17-year-old kid, $1.50 an hour was a bundle of dough, and Bob had assured the boss that we were "carpenters."

"Dad, can I borrow your tools? I got a job building concrete forms in Winchendon!"

My father looked a little amused and said, "Go ahead."

That weekend I built and sanded down great-looking toolboxes for saws, my Dad's prize hammer, brace and bit, a level, a square and other tools I barely knew how to use. When I drove to the jobsite with Bob, we jumped out of my Ford, all confident. The boss looked us up and down. He explained the work to us like we were pros and left us to our own miseries.

We sawed up 2x4s and nailed them into a passable rectangle, fastened a panel to them and thought we had turned out a pretty nice-looking product. I was feeling great about our progress, until the super strolled up.

"You boys *squared* that frame, right?"

We shook our heads. One little mistake, but we made up for it with *speed.* By the end of the day, we had "out-carpentered" most everyone else and turned in good square foundation panels. We worked 48 hours a week, with time and a half over 40 hours. With several hundred panels stacked and waiting, the boss assigned us to set the panels on top of concrete footings and start building forms over jutting plumbing pipes.

"You guys sure seem to be having a tough time gettin' the job done."

The super peered down from a catwalk above our heads, razzing us a bit, and Bob took it personally.

"This job ain't no cinch," he muttered, loud enough for the boss to hear.

It wasn't long before the super brought us news I was dreading: "You boys need to take a 25-cent cut if you want to stay on. Union carpenters'll work for less than you guys."

Bob gathered his tools in a huff and left. I just grinned and took the hardest work the supervisor and crews could dish out, while picking the brains of every good carpenter around me.

I treasured every bit of instruction I could wrest out of this first big construction job. After a few months the super laid me off, and I followed my cousin Martin Somero to the defense plant in Athol, Massachusetts. The pair of us were rejects from the military (he had broken his leg twice), but Union Twist Drill hired us in a heartbeat.

Martin, with his bum leg, stood for hours at a rolling machine, and I used my one good eye to search out tiny burrs to grind off drills, down to 1/64 of an inch! I learned to *feel* the work, and during my probation period, I ruined bunches of drills. I carried a few spoiled drills home, and a couple good ones, too, to show my folks and siblings the kind of work I was learning. I felt pretty good about myself until I asked my supervisor for a 10-cent raise.

"Don't even think about a wage increase!" he blustered. I got real indignant over his attitude.

"Then, I'm out the door, sir!"

"You go, and I'll be talking to your draft board, boy."

"You do that!" I laughed all the way to the office to collect my pay.

I drove directly to Winchendon and got hired at General Box Company. It was another job where my dexterity and speed won me a good position. I got promoted to stacking dimensional lumber on a cart after the band saw finished with it. The scream of that machine still rings in my ears. I'm sure it took the edge off my hearing for life.

About 100 men worked at General Box, and they figured that the workers had enough clout *together* to force the company to cough up a 10-cent raise. I had no idea what a "union" action meant, so I just did like all the rest of the employees.

"Guys, times are hard. Don't cut your own throats, or you'll all be out of a job," the super said, but our "union" organizer decided to call the boss' bluff.

Men started lining up to punch out. The saws all stopped running. The General Box trucks sat empty and forlorn. I was just one of the backslapping union boys, feeling pretty good about my sure-as-shootin' 10-cent raise. I watched the organizer, who held up his time card, grinning, and punched out. Ten more workers punched out ahead of me, and suddenly I stood before the time clock and jammed my card into the slot.

"Everyone punching out is FIRED!"

The supervisor stood in the doorway with a big hand waving a clipboard, red-faced. Suddenly, there was a mass exodus from the hall, and the saws started running again. I stood knee-deep in a quandary, all alone after the union organizer and his grousing cronies shuffled out the door into the street.

What did I just do?

"Hey, Seppala." The boss nodded me into a room. He closed the door. "You don't even know what a strike is, do you?"

My face must have looked pretty sheepish.

"Well, I can't hire you back today — it wouldn't be fair to the guys who stayed loyal to the company. But, you come back in a couple weeks, and you can have your job back."

Like any grateful "scab," I agreed.

I didn't head home, but went to Fitchburg and found my brother Wally. After I told him my woes, he laughed at me and helped me land a job with him at Iver Johnson Gun Factory. Maybe I couldn't carry a rifle into battle, but at least I could polish their barrels! I was paid by the "piece," rather than by the hour, so I had incentive to work my tail off.

After my two-week punishment, I didn't go back to my job at General Box. I stayed at the gun factory. It was during this time that a sermon by Pastor Mickelson played havoc with my conscience. He had been holding special meetings at our New Ipswich church, and I felt the Holy Spirit tugging at my heart: I needed to mend the breach in my relationship with Union Twist Drill.

The pastor's sermon theme went like this: The Holy Spirit alerts us to sin. It's our job to confess faults to one another to be healed. According to Revelation 1:6, a man has the right to stand in for a brother or sister and receive their confession of sin, declaring them clean in the name of Jesus and by his precious blood …"

Faults.

I remembered those silly drills I had pocketed while at Union Twist Drill, mostly my rejects, but a few that I figured were usable. Was my eternal soul in jeopardy because I had stolen these? I spoke to Pastor Mickelson about it, and he confirmed that I was forgiven for the offense. He explained how that forgiveness was an open door to restitution, when a Christian can right a wrong he or she has committed.

"You mean, I have to go back to Union Twist Drill and tell them about the good drills I (the word stuck in my throat) stole?"

"It's the right thing to do, Martin."

It was a long drive to Athol as a picture in my mind played over and over: What would the boss at UTD do with my confession? Would he laugh? Would he call the law? And how much restitution would he require?

I strode resolutely to the main office, and the secretary pointed to a man beyond an open door, who was watching me. I introduced myself and explained the job I held while working at Union Twist Drill.

"I ruined a lot of drills and took some of the rejects home to show my family, but I also took a couple of the *good* drills. I want to make restitution, sir."

A snicker from the secretary stopped me short, and I glanced her way. But the supervisor at the desk wasn't laughing. His eyes were teary. He shook his head a little and sniffed. It was a rare thing to meet a sincere 18 year old who wanted his heart to be right before his employer and his God.

"Son, don't let it burden you. Okay?"

As I drove away, I celebrated the freedom I felt after exploring "restitution," but I kicked myself about forgetting that unhardened drills were not totally worthless. I was learning that God did not expect me to be perfect. I just needed to be willing to sacrifice my pride and bulldoze any barriers that could hinder relationships. My whole guilty effort at confession had been flawed, like a batch of ruined drills, yet Jesus took my struggle and continued to shape me closer to *his* polished image.

Forming foundations

And in quiet moments, I think about the man with tears in his eyes and wonder if the sincerity of a young Christian might have nudged him a bit closer to the kingdom of God.

❧❧❧

I was 19 years old when the German government officially surrendered to General Dwight D. Eisenhower who represented our United States. President Roosevelt died in April 1945, and in August, our new president, Harry S. Truman, gave orders to drop atom bombs on two cities in Japan. The Japanese government surrendered unconditionally five days later.

At the end of World War II, Nazi extermination camps were exposed, and concentration camps in Germany and Poland were liberated and inspected by the Allies. Evidence of German atrocities shocked the world, including those of us who listened to radios in our living rooms.

Atomic bombs carried from our own American soil had disintegrated tens of thousands of living souls, and the knowledge of such devastation chilled our hearts. Any who doubted Biblical accounts of future holocausts had much to ponder: The coming unthinkable mass destruction, so vividly described in Revelation, was *possible* after all. For my family, the horrors of World War II rekindled our faith in God's prophetic word.

Mom was right: It was good to be a citizen of heaven and not tied to this corrupt world, even in our blessed "land of the free and home of the brave."

Finnish pastors had plenty to preach about in 1945. They resumed travel abroad after the war, bearing belated news of a new conflict: driving the remnant of Nazis from Finland. Soviets still brandished their sabers against Finland, and an unofficial armistice lay across the Finnish-Soviet border like a trip wire.

The best is yet to come

By joining the Nazis against the Soviet Union, Finland now shared the fate of defeated Germany, Italy and Japan. Like these Axis nations, cash reparations and massive land concessions loomed on Finland's bleak horizon.

෮෮෮

Breathtaking.

I dismounted after an intoxicating ride aboard a Harley Davidson motorcycle, clinging to the waist of my friend Ken Johanson. As soon as I found a1936 model Harley, I bought it. But Mom was not pleased.

Dick Rice had good advice for a novice rider. He knew Harleys from spokes to sprockets, and he quashed my smugness as we stood out of earshot of my concerned mother: "You *will* crash, Martin. You *will* end up in the hospital. When you feel yourself losing control, lay the bike down and hug the tank with your knees with all your strength."

I nodded gravely, picturing my first accident.

"Ride it out, don't jump off. Your bike is just like a woman: Just when you think you have her all figured out, she'll throw you for a loop!"

My 1,000 cc, 74-cubic-inch Harley Davidson needed brake work immediately. Nevertheless, it seemed that overnight a motorcycle gang surrounded me: Martin Somero bought an Indian 45, Leo Somero and my brother Edwin rode smaller versions of Harleys. I'll never forget the thrill of riding with friends or the pain that soon followed.

One evening, my sister Edna hopped aboard with me, and I followed Edwin out the driveway. After our jaunt, a 14-year-old girl from the neighborhood named Barbara Frigard wanted a ride, too, so I obliged her with a short one. Then Edna hopped back on behind me so we could catch up with Edwin who was some distance away. Barbara waved to Edna, and we sped away.

Forming foundations

I jammed the footbrake at the first sharp curve we encountered, and *nothing* happened. All my careful work on the brakes flashed through my mind, and I knew we were in trouble.

With no time to gear down, I hollered to Edna over the Harley's patented roar, "Hold tight!"

I lay the bike down as we started our 100-foot slide, and I gripped the tank with my knees, feeling the pavement grind to dirt. A tree stopped the bike dead.

Edna got up and brushed off her dress, like she had just gotten up from a nap in the weeds. I wasn't so lucky. My little sister had to lift the bike off my leg to free me. We were both glad to be alive! My leg throbbed all the way to the Frigards' house, and Semmi Frigard, Barbara's father, took me to see a doctor in Townsend. I left the shredded flesh from my knee back on asphalt and dirt. The doc cleaned out the tar from the silver dollar-sized gash and dabbed some bag balm on it.

A week later, Doc Emerson gave me more salve, but while I limped around doing chores, Dad decided I needed to see one more doctor.

He made an appointment with an old Army doctor in Jaffrey. "He's treated everything from bullet holes to dog bites. He'll know what to do."

A full 10 days after my wreck, Dr. Sweeney swore like a drill sergeant when he peeled off my bandage.

"Who's been caring for this d*** wound? You can't leave your bone exposed like that! Sit tight, boy."

Doc Sweeney grabbed up a needle and cat gut. He went to work after cleaning me up with sulfa melamine, the stuff he likely used in the war trenches. The cat gut snapped as he tried to draw my wound up tight, and I gritted my teeth. He must have noticed the color draining from my face, and he stated the obvious.

"You're passing out, son."

The best is yet to come

He left me blinking away dizziness and returned with a jigger of "medicinal" whiskey, which I gulped down, hot and fast.

With his thicker cat gut, he suddenly found his sewing "stride" and muttered to himself, "Ten days is a long time to wait before sewing this ..."

Mom would never have approved of his sloppy line of stitches, but he seemed pleased. I'm not sure if he threw back a few jiggers himself when he disappeared for a time, but he slapped a wooden brace behind my knee and wrapped it tight with a bandage.

"You come back in six weeks. It should be healed enough to take the brace off. Don't bend your leg. Let it heal up. And stay off that motorcycle!"

In six weeks the wound had healed beautifully. So I got back on my bike.

It was great fun riding my Harley to church and meeting the "gang" at services. But one particular Sunday I stayed home to make some final repairs on the cycle before taking a Sunday jaunt to Greenville. I felt a little guilty as I pulled up to church just as the service was letting out. The guys were heading down the steps with Dad and Mom in the group. We all waved goodbye, and as soon as I felt the wind in my face, I forgot all about Mom's frown.

We four bikers (with passengers behind) hit Greenville and grabbed sodas. Heading home, I brought up the rear for several miles before trying to make a pass.

Suddenly, in a split second, Leo Somero braked and made a left turn — right in front of me!

I had just enough seconds to maneuver and avoid an accident — until the Model A pulled out. Its broadside glided past my front wheel like a slow-moving ship. Donald Hill (my passenger) and I almost missed it, but my Harley's front crash bar caught the old car's bumper and yanked it clean off. Donald latched onto me for dear life, and both of us went flying end over teakettle.

Amazingly, Donald didn't get a scratch, but my pants ripped and my right knee smacked the pavement. It swelled up like a balloon as I sat in a ditch groaning.

Dick Rice's prophecy came true that day. I spent the next few days at the Burbank Hospital. And it never would have happened if I had attended church and not roared off on my Harley that fine Lord's Day.

ॐॐॐॐ

After years away at war, our Edwin was coming home.

Dad sat impatiently with the car engine running, waiting for the whole family to fill up seats. We squished together like herrings in a can, and the Ford trundled down Payson Hill Road on a mission.

Suddenly Alvina squealed, "There he is!"

Actually, it was Roland Goddard's car slowing to a stop, and Dad pulled over, too. Edwin flung open a car door and stood like the soldier on a recruiter's poster, handsome and grinning ear to ear. Mom ran into his outstretched arms, followed by his sisters.

Free for all.

My big brother ran a gauntlet of Seppalas, hugging, kissing and wrestling until Dad grabbed him in a final bear hug. He crammed Edwin into our herring can, and we all headed home. Edwin tossed his Army duffle bag on the kitchen floor, and while supper was being prepared, he tried to catch up on all the hometown news. That evening at the table, we studied the ecstasy on Edwin's face as he wolfed down a special meal Mom knew he loved.

Before bed, our long-absent son and brother strolled outside to make sure his old 1935 Ford still sat in the weeds.

The best is yet to come

He'd been dreaming about the old Ford for months, hoping that it still grew moss behind Dad's barn.

In 1946, our family celebrated Edwin's honorable discharge from the U.S. Army, the same year that our Federation of Apostolic Lutheran Church convened a convention at New York Mills, Minnesota. We kids and our cousins had bees buzzing in our bonnets about a road trip to Minnesota, so Edwin gathered up wrenches his first week home. He hauled the '35 into the barn and tore it down, piece by piece, then replaced the engine and all necessary parts.

I acquired a few gallons of cheap blue enamel paint and sprayed it on, my first time painting a car body. Bluebird was ready to fly!

Our chauffeur wore a grin as his eyes met Mom's teary ones. Leo, Martin and Philip Somero hung out the windows of Leonard Somero's '36 Ford, and Mom stood on the porch with Dad, satisfied that her boy was home and surrounded by "friendly forces."

Alvina, Edna and I squeezed into the '35 Bluebird Ford and ate dust from Leonard for a while. Then we urged Edwin to pass him. We were heading to our first "big meeting" of Lutherans since the war had begun.

Edwin might have felt like a prisoner under interrogation on the first leg of our trip. We plied him with questions about the wonders of the exotic places he had experienced, like Persia.

In Detroit, we bunked with Walter and Ina Mae, great Finnish friends, then resumed our journey to New York Mills.

Boys outnumbered Lutheran girls three-to-one back home, and at convention, it seemed we had crossed over to Paradise. Everywhere, dozens of dresses and young smiles! And the most heavenly aspect: Nearly all of these girls would pass muster with our mothers, because they were Lutheran and Finnish.

We had barely registered with the housing committee and made sure our sisters were settled in with a nice Finnish couple, when I started tossing our luggage into the back seat of Leonard's '36.

"Bet Leo and I get some girls before you guys do!"

Edwin frowned. "Get my car back in one piece," he said and chuckled as he strode off to find some old friends. I jumped behind the steering wheel, speeding off with Leo, away from the convention.

"There!"

Two tall, slender young ladies strolled along the sidewalk, and our Bluebird fluttered up next to them — which they absolutely ignored.

"Don't think they saw us ..." Leo said.

"How could they *miss* us? They're going into that diner ..."

We slammed doors, straightened our ties and plopped down beside them at their table. The two sisters, Marj and Marie Niemitalo, were relieved that we charming "hoodlums" were good Lutheran boys from the New York Mills Convention. As for a ride in our big Finnish Bluebird: no contest. We met up with Leonard and Martin with grinning trophies, and they had girls with them, too: Helen Tapio and Doris Suomi. The girls took the place of our luggage, which Leo and Martin had pitched into an outhouse.

Every Finnish Lutheran in the New York Mills area had overnight visitors for the next few days. Young men slept in haylofts, and young ladies enjoyed hospitality in safe Finnish homes. Hay and blankets never felt so wonderful, as we boys crowded into a farmer's barn for the night.

Convention began on a Thursday and lasted until Sunday, three grand services a day. Our song leader opened with a hymn, and an elder prayed a blessing over convention activities. Our voices rose in youthful praise in the next song, and the daily convention preacher read a Bible text, the theme of his upcoming message.

In our simple, uniform Lutheran order of service, we young

adults opened our hearts to Jesus. Gifted elders preached, and each one could easily have filled the pulpit in any of our Apostolic home churches. Our souls absorbed God's word through strong approved Lutheran roots.

Like flour in Finnish cupboards, the staple in every message was our need to repent often (openly confirm our change of direction), due to inescapable contact with evil in the world we lived in. One of our speakers was a former soldier, like my brother Edwin, who had taken up arms to halt the holocaust from reaching American shores. This young man's preaching struck my heart.

He hung a billboard on obviously bad behavior: drunkenness, lying, stealing, adultery, swearing and hatred, to name a few. In 1946, bad conduct still had a name that *everyone*, rich or poor, educated or illiterate, knew: It was called SIN.

This young soldier captured our hearts as he marched across the stage. He preached about God's Son, Jesus, who bled on the cross to give us peace and victory. Heaven was our destination, but "eternity" began the moment we gave our lives to God. We could live a clean and happy life guided by the Holy Spirit.

Refreshed.

We drove home from the convention excited about the future. Young men and women at New York Mills mirrored a new national hopefulness. The United States was poised to become the greatest industrial power ever known, and we children of immigrant Finnish farmers were proud Americans. We felt like we were part of God's plan.

Our bluebird perched for the night at the home of Wayne Kinnunen, a new friend we met at the convention, brother of Marj and Marie, the girls we had followed into the diner. Wayne became a lifelong friend.

To my relief and great anticipation, I found that there were plenty of Finnish girls available, for I had decided it was time to find a wife. But I had no clue that a girl down the road had set her cap for me.

And the most ambitious Seppala in New Hampshire didn't stand a chance.

❧❧❧

None of us Seppala brothers lacked good Christian pals in our Finnish community, but most of them were boys. Girls in the Rindge area had the pick of the marriageable young bucks, and they tossed up chaff until the truest of hearts remained. We bachelors were tempted to date outside of our faith and church, but parents had the last word, especially if we lived at home.

Our Apostolic Lutheran Church served Finnish families in very practical ways: We heard the gospel taught by many good men and women, and we surrounded ourselves with like-minded Christian folk. For the unmarried, every service became a venue to find the finest grist for the mill. And most important to the families, our mothers used church to observe the conduct of those who might court a daughter or flirt with a son.

Little Barbara Frigard loved my 1941 Ford. At 14, she was a cute girl, way too young for me, but interesting. She displayed a headstrong mindset, unlike other girls, a no-nonsense quality that seemed out of character for a young woman her age. I hadn't really noticed Barbara until the day she stood on the running board of my '41, looking over the interior — or looking *me* over. I was a little confused as to which it was. She was the kid who had always begged for a ride on my motorcycle.

One day, as I sat in the church parking lot waiting for Arthur, Barbara jumped into my car and slammed the door.

"Hey, whatcha doing?" I said, a little amused.

"Where we goin', Marty?"

I sat there, flummoxed, but her words sparked my

cylinders. Suddenly the neighbor girl seemed *older.* She must have matured sometime when I was away working. Then, the next thing I knew, I heard that she was dating someone.

So was I. In fact, my girlfriend and I had been discussing family matters.

"I'm planning to have a lot of kids."

"Really, Marty? How many?"

"About a dozen ..."

Silence, then she snickered. "Bury me right now!"

That was our last date.

Barbara had turned 15 and kept coming back to my mind, so I decided to take her out for a soda, just to settle the bothersome issue once and for all.

"How about a ride and an ice cream?"

"I need to ask Daddy."

I pictured stern Semmi Frigard frowning about me in his easy chair, in his big brick house. I fidgeted, listening hard, and finally I heard Barbara tip-tapping up to the kitchen phone again.

"When you coming?"

It was early evening, and her parents set a curfew before we left. I had no idea that Barbara had promised to date my cousin that same evening. She passed off the task of telling the disappointed boy that she "couldn't make it after all" before she drove off with me. Our "date" was hot news on the Finnish grapevine the next week, and it dawned on me — it never was my nifty '41 that little Barbara Frigard had been checking out. It was me.

Going steady.

The year of Barbara's 16th birthday trotted past as though we were racing the streets of Rindge in a dapper horse-drawn surrey. It seemed like we had known each other our whole lives, which indeed was the case. Thoughts of marriage consumed both of us: starting a big, wonderful family, working hard together, building our own house and … we had acres of love to share!

Still, the question remained in my heart: Would Barbara Frigard really say yes to such a driven young man as I?

The day I planned to settle that big question, I bought a solitaire diamond ring, and all the way to her house I rehearsed how I would tell her that I loved her. She was waiting on the front steps as I rumbled to a stop in the '41 and honked. We were on the way to Art and Ida's house for a "sing and eat" gathering and were running a little late.

It had been harder than I thought to choose a diamond that I could afford, and butterflies roiled my stomach as Barbara hopped in beside me.

"Martin Seppala, where have you been? We're going to walk into Art and Ida's and everyone will be looking at us like …"

"Barbara, uh … here." I fumbled in my coat pocket for the little blue box and handed it to her, like it was half a sandwich from my lunchbox. "This is the reason I was late."

She untied the delicate bow, lifted the lid and the diamond glinted in the moonlight. Her pretty mouth stopped pouting. Her face brightened like I had lit a lantern in the cab, and she talked non-stop all the way to the song service. By the time we sang the last hymn, drank the last coffee and ate our last dessert, everyone knew about my intentions *and* her diamond. I had "the talk" with Semmi Frigard, and our engagement became official.

I had no idea that I needed to consult her about important decisions *before* we tied the knot, but I found out. Roland Goddard wanted to buy my '41 Ford, and I really liked a long cool 12-cylinder Lincoln Continental I knew was for sale. After our deals were struck, I lumbered up to the Frigards' to show off my new prize.

"What's this? Where's *our* little Ford?"

After that, a storm brewed behind Barbara's eyes whenever

she sat in my big beautiful Lincoln. She simply refused to see things the right way.

Thankfully, I had little to do with her complex wedding blueprint, although I did get to choose my best man, Roland Goddard (who relished Barbara's glare whenever he parked the '41 near my Lincoln). I also chose my groomsmen: Wayne Hoyt, Hjalmer Aho and my brother Edwin.

Barbara chose her only sister, Elmi, to be matron of honor and my sisters, Alvina and Evelyn, and Nancy Somero to be bridesmaids. Pastor Emanuel Aho married us, and our New Ipswich Apostolic Lutheran Church overflowed with people, gifts and laughter.

I was standing apart from the crowd, talking with my dad, when I heard Barbara screech. Suddenly several young men hustled my new wife outside! Car doors slammed — and she was *gone*. Stolen right out from under my nose! A few other big Finns thought I had a date with a nearby creek, and they hauled me off.

It took all my strength to keep from getting a full dunking, though I had it coming. I had incited a kidnapping of Eino Ojala, and he had ended up floundering in a lake after he came back from eloping. He and others had been plotting my payback plunge for a long time.

It was late at night before we all left the church, the food and our wonderful friends. I drove to Ashby with Barbara cuddling close, and we spent our first night at a rented cabin, worn out. The next morning we ate a very special breakfast at Mumu and Papa's house (my new in-laws, the Frigards), and then, like two sparrows uncaged, we sped to our honeymoon in Washington, D.C. Of course, I drove my Lincoln Continental, which Barbara mercilessly compared to the '41 Ford until I started to miss it, too.

After our honeymoon, we moved into one side of the Frigards' brick house, now a duplex, and I continued my job at

Forming foundations

Iver Johnson Gun Factory in Fitchburg, polishing gun barrels. As an untested husband, my first marital challenge signaled a lifelong struggle — to rein in my selfish impatience. Barbara never seemed to "hurry" enough for me.

"I really need to help plant Mom's garden today."

Barbara's eyes shone, utterly excited about tilling and planting, a boring job that I had been required to do most of my life. I had a whole sweaty Saturday's worth of soil preparation ahead, so I paced while she cleaned up the house. After a few minutes, I came to the end of my foolish young rope.

"I'll be back after a while. Go ahead and work around here. I'll come back and pick you up a little later."

As I drove away, I figured that we were efficiently killing two birds with a single stone. I was satisfied with one of my first decisions as a husband in the first month of our wedded bliss.

Dad, Arthur and Edwin were just pulling out of the drive as I pulled in.

"We're heading to Maine for fireworks. Wanna come? Can't get any in New Hampshire, they're still outlawed."

Road trip!

I scrunched into the car and added up the time I would be gone.

Three hours up, and three hours back — the same amount of time I'd use to till the garden today, which I could put off. Besides, Barbara said she wanted to help me in the garden, didn't she?

But the closer we got to home, the more my conscience bubbled with doubt. I remembered my last words — "I'll pick you up a *little* later" — and gulped.

Dad was driving sooo *slowly!*

At home, my brothers stretched and rifled through their fireworks.

"Come in for a piece of pie?" Mom hollered from the porch, but I waved as I sped off to pick up Wayne Hoyt. Surely my

The best is yet to come

dear wife would be reasonable when she saw I had a friend with me. And I carried a luscious peace offering to the door, where she tearfully waited.

"Look, here are some strawberries ... for *you*."

"Martin Seppala, you can KEEP your old strawberries!"

It was a long silent evening after I took Wayne home, and I learned a hard lesson, one that I forgot more than once over the years of our marriage. Even today it's sometimes hard to send that selfish fireworks-loving boy inside me packing.

࿂࿂࿂

But the "boy" in a man vanishes when he nearly loses his first love.

I felt so powerless when Barbara took sick while carrying our son Daniel. Shuffled from doctor to doctor, no one had the answer to why she could keep nothing in her stomach. She suffered with fever and was injected with penicillin multiple times a day. After two full weeks, the fever finally broke.

Nine months.

I continued to work at Iver Johnson Gun Factory, hardly able to concentrate on the job. When the day finally came for her delivery, I studied the girl I had married, weak and undernourished. She barely looked pregnant.

At the hospital, I was shunted off to a waiting room and forgotten. Hours dragged on, with no one to tell me anything. I prayed like I had never prayed before.

I could lose them both.

"Mr. Seppala?" A nurse came in smiling. "You have a baby boy, a little small at 4 ½ pounds, but healthy."

"My wife? How's Barbara?" I felt hot tears coming.

The nurse took a breath and looked concerned. "She'll need lots of care. Especially bed rest."

My wife's body had given up every ounce of nutrition it

86

produced to help Daniel survive, which became Barbara's lifelong recipe to follow as long as she lived. She always gave more than anyone expected, and God multiplied every ounce of her effort to sustain others — as wife, mother and friend.

Barbara weighed less during the nine months she carried Daniel than before she was pregnant. Moreover, after her delivery, doctors worried over the condition of her mind. In the hospital, she sometimes lost control of her senses. They advised me to have her examined at a mental hospital in Worchester, but I balked at even considering the possibility.

"I'm taking you home, hon."

Plenty of help awaited us, and the very next day in her own bed, she was in her right mind and *eating*. Baby Daniel came home soon after, and with the loving care of my Finnish family, my young wife and my firstborn son gained weight and strength.

My faith was tested during these harrowing days. I had never loved with more intensity or knocked harder upon the gates of heaven for answers. I believe I prayed within God's will, and the Holy Spirit poured new footings into my soul upon which I began to build my spiritual life.

Some physicians advised us to refrain from having more children for at least five years, but we were young and simply trusted in the Author of Life. Eighteen months after Daniel's birth, Sandy was born, a healthy, chubby girl. Fourteen months later, Annie came into our lives. And in the following years, Barbara bore 14 more children without complications. Seventeen isn't a round figure, but it turned out to be a most blessed number for Barbara and me.

ॡॡॡ

For months, I had been coming home from work with sharp wire nubs imbedded in my chest. One day I told Semmi about it, and he shook his head. "Martin, just quit the gun factory. I know a contractor who'll likely hire you."

Mr. Raatikainen, the contractor Semmi worked for, hired me on the spot. The work I had done in Winchendon, setting concrete forms, was a godsend. I understood the first-phase ground-up principle in construction: Make it square and level! And on this first job, I gave my opinion about a top plate that looked as crooked as a dog's hind leg.

"What should we do?" The boss' son-in-law stood scratching his head.

I sketched out a plan to fix the problem, and we followed it. When Mr. Raatikainen heard about my initiative, he set me on a new job building a house, starting with the foundation wall. We used a little underpowered cement mixer, and I still feel the ache when I think of the hundreds of buckets of concrete we hauled up ladders to pour into forms.

We built the house, though, bottom to top, siding and shingles. In this first home construction job, God granted me a wealth of knowledge in the trades. Unlike factory work, I loved creating a fine structure, knowing that I was part of a project I could see and be proud of.

And the 8 year old sent by his mother to rent a blueberry field began to plot his course toward creating architectural wonders he could never have fathomed at the ripe old age of 25.

Father and Mother, Gus & Annie Seppala

Old church on Poor Farm Road, New Ipswich, New Hampshire.

Apostolic Lutheran Church in downtown New Ipswich.

Rindge schoolhouse (Thanks to the Rindge Historical Society)

Family - Back: Martin (about 9 years old), Wally, Arthur, Edwin
Front: Alvina, Evelyn, Edna

Annie Seppala (mother), Gus Seppala (father), Arthur (brother),
Sisters in front: Alvina, Elaine, Edna, Evelyn (About 1938)

Dressed for Sunday church in 1943. Leonard Somero, Roland Goddard, Leo Somero, Martin Seppala (17 years old), Hjalmer Aho, Martin Somero

Seppala home place on Payson Hill Road in Rindge, New Hampshire. Sister Elaine pulling children in wagon (chicken house in back).

Martin and Barbara at the Seppala home place (barn in background).

Martin and Barbara's wedding picture - May 29, 1948

Chapter four
Endings and beginnings

"How Greeeeeat Thou Art!"

Al Mattson and Eddie Haapoja paused for their hymn crescendo with grins, then resumed their *tat-tat-tat*, nailing down roof sheathing atop one of our houses in Fitchburg.

I had been working with a fine carpenter, George Berglund, for several months when a Jewish developer, Mr. Adler, from Boston bought George and me lunch, then proposed this: "I have several houses to build on properties in Fitchburg. Can you gentlemen supply the management of construction if I provide all your materials? I'll pay you for each completed house, but withhold 20 percent until you drive the last nail. This is insurance that the jobs will be finished to my specifications."

That same evening, George and I sat down at Semmi's kitchen table, scribbling and scheming late into the night, until we scratched out figures *we* could live with and a schedule and price Mr. Adler could live with.

Sold.

Mr. Adler's building plans were straightforward, and the next week he wrote us checks for the shopping list of materials we submitted. We immediately contracted local men with equipment to dig footings for the first houses, and we hired Al and Eddie as framers. This was my maiden voyage into the contracting business. East Coast horizons lay before me like unexplored territory!

How many other developers needed honest men to ramrod their construction jobs?

I loved business management from the first day I grabbed a clipboard. At dawn I bounded out the door (after breakfast and

The best is yet to come

a smooch from Barbara), ready to set rafters or boss a crew. Jovial and driven, I dug ditches or walked wall plates like I was one of the hired hands. I trotted off to meetings (I hated to be late), and with my artesian well of enthusiasm, the expression "Let's do it now!" infused my work. The oft-repeated phrase irritated many, but guided me in decades of overseeing construction-related businesses. Within months, more than 30 of Mr. Adler's houses were popping up in his subdivisions, like mushrooms after a summer cloudburst.

On this first big contracting job, my dad's moral support was the cornerstone of my self-confidence. He visited our jobsite one day, and I read the satisfaction in his eyes as he sighted down each wall.

"Looks pretty straight."

He stuck out his jaw in admiration and nodded to my mother, who smiled indulgently.

Al and Eddie were nailing asphalt shingles on one side of the house, and Dad grabbed a few, then slapped them into position. The young men glanced at each other, grinning, and I couldn't help but feel proud, watching my father, a little gray now, so precise and nimble.

"Need another hand?" Dad asked as he started laying shingles out for me. I was fast, but Dad lined up shingles quicker than anyone I ever saw.

Sixty years later, I see my father and I working shoulder to shoulder as if it were *moments ago*. On this sunny morning, God allowed my father to harvest a little fruit from his own vineyard by sharing work with the son whose character he helped shape. Leaning on the car, in quiet repose, Mom studied us, sensing the fulfilling embrace of two strong wills. I had no idea that these precious moments were falling like grains of sand upon eternal shores.

"Might come out and help you boys, Martin," Dad said, and I kept nailing.

Endings and beginnings

"We could use you," I said, matter-of-factly.

Mom waved as Dad opened the car door for her. I barely noticed them driving off as I hammered on.

A week later, Barbara and I helped Papa Semmi on a building project, and Dad and Mom pulled up while we nailed down a floor. My father loved Barbara like his own daughter and treated her just the same.

He observed Barbara working for a bit, then asked her, "Shall I get you a shovel? It might be a lot easier to hit those nails ..."

Barbara's hazel eyes snapped at him, which Dad enjoyed thoroughly, like he had hit *his* nail squarely.

It was the last time we would laugh together with my father.

Mom called me at Semmi's the next day, and I could hear a shudder in her voice as she tried to maintain control.

"If you want to see your father alive, Martin, you need to get to the Burbank Hospital right away."

Barbara hurriedly gathered up the kids while I rang a nurses' station at the hospital and inquired about Gus Seppala's condition.

"I'm very sorry ... Mr. Seppala has expired, sir."

I held the phone dumbly as Barbara asked me what was wrong.

"Dad's *gone.*"

Barbara cried for both of us on the way to the farmhouse, where family was gathering to support Mom. I drove in silence, feeling a sudden fracture in my self-confidence, like a crack in a bearing wall.

Gone.

At the memorial service, everyone remembered Gus Seppala for his innovative ways and helping hands. I recalled his bear hugs and treasured his grousing about my chores — I wished I could look him in the eye one last time and tell him how much I loved and respected him.

The best is yet to come

It was because of his love for Annie that Gus first came to the little church at New Ipswich and gave his heart to Jesus. Like shoe tacks at the factory where he wooed her, Annie lost count of so many precious memories. His smile distracted her even now, and she could almost hear his gentle yet strong voice singing especially for her again: "Do you remember the path where we met, long, long ago, long ago ..."

In evenings, when they were alone, snuggling with him in his Model A. Stuffing his lunchbox with bread and cheese. Gus' face livened Annie's heart as he held his newborn boys and girls in the house they built together. As a husband and father, he had been a quiet Christian, living an honest life, unadorned and reliable.

He would be proud of his family: His grieving children gathered, no longer chicks crowding beneath protective wings. All were capable and strong — breaking fresh ground along with Annie in a world without her beloved Gus.

As for my father's most self-assured and competent son, Dad's death at such a young age weighed upon me. At unexpected times, an inexplicable anxiety enfolded me like a suffocating blanket. While leveling a wall or bolting down a bottom plate with George, Al and Eddie, sometimes my father's agony would assault me, squeezing my chest with an iron grip. When these panic attacks came, I empathized with my dad in his last seconds on earth.

Sometimes dizziness plagued me. My heart thrashed wildly, and my chest felt tender over my ribs. I would suddenly kneel and wait for it to pass.

"Get me to a doctor," I told Al Mattson one day, and when he parked at the doctor's office, I leaped out and ran inside. In the waiting room, I hollered that I was dying and that I needed to see someone.

A doctor moved his cold stethoscope from place to place on my aching chest, and suddenly he stopped, like he had come to the end of his moves on a checkerboard. He shrugged.

"Son, there's nothing wrong with your heart. You're as healthy as a horse."

"But the pain ..."

"You're a bundle of nerves, Mr. Seppala. It happens sometimes when you've been under a lot of pressure."

Nerves? I felt like I was dying!

Some weeks later, in the middle of the night, I lay in bed while my heart throbbed like a jackhammer. Quietly I left Barbara sleeping and drove myself to Keene Hospital. A doctor examined me and gave me the same diagnosis: I was a healthy young buck, suffering from a nervous condition.

When I arrived home, I "confessed" about my peculiar panic attacks to Barbara — the hardest confession I had ever spoken aloud. I felt so ashamed and weak as a husband, but I detected only compassion in Barbara's hazel eyes. A brace of trust strengthened our relationship from that day on.

Still, month after month, I tried to keep my dizziness and sudden palpitating heart "attacks" to myself — and there were dozens of them.

One day I felt an attack coming on, and I finally came to the end of my rope. If Jesus intended to take me to heaven like my father, let it be NOW.

I peeled off my sweater and slammed the door behind me. It was late evening, and Barbara was getting the kids in bed when I started to *run*. Miles? Hours? I have no idea how far or long it was, but I expected to die in "forward gear," if that was God's will.

It wasn't. In fact, I felt the cure taking place in my soul as I flopped to the ground, huffing, praying and laughing at myself. Nerves, phooey! More than a year had passed since my first attacks. That day I threw out my panic episodes, like slurry in a ditch. My father's death had triggered the condition, but God ended it for me right there.

The best is yet to come

Our Fitchburg project ended, too, and Mr. Adler met us at his office for the final payoff. He owed us for the last few houses, plus several thousand dollars as the 20 percent promised upon completion. I was tense as we sat down at the table. He handed me the largest check I had ever seen, and the surprise on my face amused the elderly Jewish man.

I grinned and said, "It's more than I expected, sir."

"Why is that? You fulfilled your contract."

We had little recourse in those exhilarating days of our youth, if someone of means decided to hornswoggle us. We had no grasp of attorney-speak or small print. A few men took advantage of me during youthful ignorance. But from the beginning, I committed to honest dealings with honest men. When I made a promise to a man, I also made it to God himself. My prayer was to surround myself with others who lived by the same moral code as I did, knowing that God was hard at work on my behalf.

After the Fitchburg job, I was out of work for a time, but Barbara, the kids and I rode around in style. I bought a beautiful 1950 Ford for $1,200 bucks.

❧❧❧

"Martin, you've got to do better work than that!"

I felt heat rising on the back of my neck, and it *wasn't* sunburn. Einari Ojala hammered his cat's paw into a window frame to extract a nail I had driven. I hadn't noticed that the edge of the frame split slightly, when I used a #8 nail instead of a #6.

"Try it again," Einari groused and stomped away.

I had taken employment with Einari and Eino Ojala as carpenter for Mr. Bowron, a local contractor. It was the first time since working with my dad that my "best" never seemed to be quite up to standard. Einari studied every move I made, like a hen studying an anthill. He wasn't about to let my work reflect badly on him or his brother.

His attitude gnawed on my ego, but Einari was the most efficient carpenter I had ever seen. I made it my goal to gut it out and learn all I could, leaving a few chunks of my pride on subfloors along the way. By the time our job with Mr. Bowron ended, we three were great friends. As craftsmen and Christians, their excellence in workmanship spilled over from their careful spiritual lives serving God.

Barbara and the kids needed a larger house, and *I* needed space for a growing yard full of projects. It was time to build our own house, and Semmi obliged us by giving up 3 acres near him for our first home. A trash-filled block basement remained intact on the property. The wood structure, however, had deteriorated beyond repair, and I had a brilliant idea.

Why not just cut *one* corner and set the whole trash heap aflame? I was too busy to haul away garbage, and all my work would be finished in a single giant puff of smoke! I glanced up and down Richardson Road for traffic, then doused the pile with five gallons of gasoline. The rubbish was well-contained inside the block foundation, and barely a breeze ruffled my hair that morning. The pungent odor of gasoline wafted about me, however, an unheeded warning against impatience. I tossed in a match and backed away to watch.

The inferno surprised me.

Hotter and hotter the fire burned, climbing out of the cellar and onto the dry grass along the foundation wall. Orange flame slithered toward an old shed several feet from the basement, then hungrily latched onto it. I hopped about stomping at burning grass. I slapped down embers of floating paper lighting on leaves. But the flames kept *gathering*.

An engine suddenly roared behind me, and I recognized the driver of a school bus full of kids, pointing at the blaze from

The best is yet to come

windows. The school bus driver, Mr. Randal, was a fire official for the city of Rindge, and he accosted me with an air of importance.

"Seppala, you don't have a burn permit, do you? I'm ringing the fire bell to get some help and charge you for our work!"

"I don't have the money. Give me a little time!"

Another vehicle pulled up, and I thanked God under my breath. Some friends jumped out and grabbed shovels from the back of their trucks before trotting over to help. Mr. Randal hesitated, then, after a few more caustic comments, he carried my audience away. He drove past later to make certain the fire was out.

As for my stubborn trash heap — year upon year of blackened cans, cardboard, engine parts and household garbage still layered the foundation floor, waiting for me to haul it all away. Goodhearted Eddie and Al helped me shovel the basement clean, but I had to hire a truck for several dump runs.

The Finnish credit union in Fitchburg took into account my drive and reputation for honesty when I applied for my first mortgage. With $5,000 at 5 percent interest, I bought a load of lumber to frame up Barbara's dream home. Three bedrooms and one bathroom. Dining room, living room, kitchen and a fireplace. HOME. Outside we built a sauna (of course), a garage and a breezeway.

Our beloved Richardson Road home, built atop that old basement, set our family on solid footing as I dreamt of lofty enterprises. Now we were ready for a *bunch* more children, and Samuel was born in 1953, then Debbie the next year. They loved each other like little twins, and we reveled in God's provision for our new beginnings.

🙖🙖🙖

Endings and beginnings

In the 1950s, a man's word still carried weight among American businessmen. Whether the blueprint lined out a room addition or a high-rise, attorneys stood in the background of transactions while we shook hands over contracts. Not so today, as corporate protection is primary, and *trust* is laughed out of boardrooms.

The Aho kids frolicked in our living room with our children, while Barbara and Elmi sat in the kitchen talking over the sermon we had enjoyed not an hour ago.

Hjalmer, a stocky Finn with sandy hair, commiserated with me on the porch, away from the noisy kids. Both of us had been laid off from interim carpentry jobs and were searching for new opportunities.

"What we need is a loan, Hjalmer. Semmi has a lot he would deed us, if we had the money to build a house to sell."

Hjalmer got distracted as a baby started crying inside the house. He half-rose, then sat down again. "You got her, Elmi?"

The crying stopped, and Hjalmer smiled, like he had just remembered a favorite dessert.

"Martin, you know Mr. Johnson? My brother Ed works with him all the time. I know him fairly well. I think he might be someone to talk to."

We hatched our plan, and the next morning, I picked him up before driving to Johnson's Lumber Company. We left the old lumberman's office, with our loan to build our first house. It was the first time I had even met the man, but the Seppala and Aho families had been doing business in the area for many years. Semmi deeded over a piece of ground, with our promise to pay him when we sold the house we built — our first spec home.

To keep costs down we purchased lumber from a Townsend, Massachusetts, sawmill, not Johnson's, which likely rankled him. But he gave his two young family men a lot of slack in their first project. He loaned money for the materials we *didn't* buy from him *and* paid us wages monthly, so that we could survive while waiting for the house to sell.

This was a truly ground-up spec home: septic, well, foundation, structure. During the three months of dawn-to-dusk work, Roland Goddard married my little sister Evelyn, then bought the house before it was even finished — for $7,500. After paying back Mr. Johnson and Semmi, we turned a profit with an eye to the future of our fledgling company: Seppala & Aho.

Our next building project, on a lot near the Frigards' house, acted like a magnet for new opportunities. Mrs. Saari wanted a house built on Ashby State Road, and a young couple in Fitchburg heard about us and wanted us to bid on construction of their home. Night and day we dug footing and poured stem walls, framed and contracted others to dig wells or set septic tanks.

We then contracted to build several more houses in Fitchburg, and good men expressed a desire to work with us. We hired Bill Aho, Hjalmer's brother, and started buying heavy equipment to keep him and the others busy: first a dump truck to haul fill, then a backhoe to dig footings. Supervising these projects ran me ragged from town to town, so we hired Edwin to help supervise.

We made our first dent in the commercial construction market when we bid on a large church addition in Townsend. Hjalmer and I looked over the blueprints, and I immediately noticed problems.

"Do these joists seem a little light for the span to you?"

"Yup. Better let the architect know."

I did and still came in with the lowest bid, even after upgrading the thickness of lumber to carry the load across the area.

We got the job — and needed more help.

"Who are you guys, anyway?" people asked, so we came up

with an official name: Seppala & Aho Construction Company, based out of our new "office" in New Ipswich.

My little sister Elaine had a head for figures, so she kept our books in a corner nook of the Hjalmer's house. Thank God for my little sister. "You guys are going bankrupt, Martin!" Elaine exclaimed. "You MUST raise your prices."

We did and in the nick of time as we finished up the church job. The architect whom I had warned about the wrong thickness of joist lumber called us to bid on another commercial building, a dream come true for me.

The architect extended his hand. "I'm figuring a job for a Chevrolet dealership in Ayers, Massachusetts, Martin. I'm not forgetting how you headed off a big problem in that church job."

We landed the Chevy garage contract, while working on several high-class homes, colonial style, which were way beyond my expertise. I called Einari, and he supervised these jobs, including the house that "smiled."

Tell most construction men you want a house to "smile," and he'll either look like he doesn't get the joke, or he'll tell you to find someone else to build it.

But I was exuberant. I never blinked when Mrs. Preston and her architect explained that they wanted the house to look like it grew from the ground like a plant. And she wanted it to *smile* at her when she drove into her driveway.

No one in all of Dublin, New Hampshire (or the East Coast, for that matter), would have a home like it. When we finished, the Prestons' massive home seemed to invite you inside when you came near. We used huge field stones for their fireplace and set a picture window that faced Mount Monadnock. The "bear" den was designed with a low doorway of mortar and field stones that opened into a wonderful library.

One morning, as I was helping build concrete forms in a ditch, the architect came by and hollered at me to come up.

The best is yet to come

"The general contractor shouldn't be shoveling mud in a ditch. You're the boss now, Martin!"

I stood around and jawed with him as long as he stayed, but when he left, I hopped down into the ditch again. And you might say I've *stayed* in that ditch, working alongside the men I hire. I still can saw a straight line, and rubbing shoulders with CEOs has never changed me.

I hired the best crews I could find for the big garage project, and Hjalmer oversaw each operation, including watching the iron workers squaring beams and bar joists. The Chevrolet Garage, complete with showroom, office, parts department and service areas, ended up the talk of the Ayer community. With the profit we cleared, we poured money into acquiring more heavy equipment.

Untested Seppala & Aho had quickly leaped the chasm from tract housing to million-dollar commercial ventures. We had no clue that while gaining footing on this "big money" side, our silhouette framed us as a beautiful target.

Jobs began stacking up, like cinderblocks in a splendid foundation. Even before we finished the Chevrolet Garage, we landed a fresh bid on a motel.

Do it now.

We finished the dirt work in a week and started setting forms for footings. I scheduled a concrete pour with Keating Concrete Ready Mix in Fitchburg, and we watched with anticipation as the first truck lumbered to our worksite — then parked at the street.

We stood waving them over, but they didn't budge. It was the first time I felt the intangible power of "pickets." About 10 men, carrying signs, laughed and talked around the Ready Mix trucks, like they were old cronies. My men all stopped to watch, while I fumed.

"Oh, come on! Why don't they just roll over here and dump their batches?"

Endings and beginnings

We discovered that the concrete plant in Fitchburg was a closed union shop, adhering strictly to labor union rules. The stubborn picketers were acting as a "wall" between our non-union jobsite and the outside union world.

"D*** Scabs!" The picketers shouted and waved signs at us, while the trucks turned around to leave.

"We better call someone who knows about these unions, Martin," Hjalmer said, shaking his head, and then sent some of the concrete finishers home.

The local attorney had no experience with unions and directed us to Washington, D.C., where an expensive lawyer started a lawsuit against the union. But I couldn't wait for a judgment. I found an "open-shop" concrete company in Worchester, Massachusetts, a shop that didn't mind crossing a picket line. They mixed our concrete soupy so it would last the distance and not "set up."

The picketers remained at our gate, and we struggled to find open-shop plumbing and electrical companies, welders and carpenters, until our attorney lowered the boom. A judgment was issued against this union for stopping our work, and the picketers were banned from our site.

I was pretty vocal about how un-American picketing was — against men who just wanted to make a living and owners who needed to grow their company. Before the attorney left for Washington, he took me aside. He was an older gentleman, and I respected his advice.

"Martin, don't be too mad at the union boys."

He told me about how the Rockefellers owned coal fields in the Midwest and barely paid wages enough to take care of miners' families. The miners lived in squalid coal towns, and when the workers joined the union and tried to force the supervisors to consider the poor working conditions and give a wage increase, Rockefeller used his influence to send state government men to break the strike.

The best is yet to come

The clash left more than 18 men dead when it was over. Giant corporations have one aim in life: to make money for their shareholders — and it is never enough. Truly, the love of money is the root of all evil, as scripture tells us.

I wonder what Grandfather Gus Seppala would have advised me, as a Finnish coal miner breathing black dust in the tunnels of Rock Springs, Wyoming.

After 30 years of hiring workmen for my construction projects, I've never forgotten that attorney's account of how things can get out of hand when a man feels his livelihood is threatened. I left my bitterness at the foot of Jesus' cross, but struggled with anger sometimes over dirty tricks the unions often stooped to, rather than upfront legal confrontation.

☙☙☙

Sometimes a young man's reach exceeds his grasp ...

I had heard that chicken farming was profitable, and I had enough land at my Richardson property to build a fine three-story broiler "condo." There, I could fatten up 5,000 or more cluckers at a time.

I installed Plexiglass windows in our chicken mansion, so that the hens received proper sunlight. In about 12 weeks, my fryers attained marketable weight. Buyers from the slaughterhouse rolled into our yard like grim reapers, snatched up my unwilling, noisy fryers and crated them for a ride to the butcher. They paid us by the "poultry pound."

As the months passed, I automated an electric lighting schedule, the single most life-sustaining issue in chicken farming, besides feeding. Chickens are drawn to light and warmth. Large, unruly congregations can suffocate if they stampede to a single lighted section of the chicken house. So I mounted incandescent bulbs evenly all over their residence to keep them thinned out and healthy.

Endings and beginnings

But one day, my carefully programmed system failed. Due to my erratic daily schedule (church meetings, family get-togethers, business appointments and overseeing jobs), I bungled the "timing" for proper chicken illumination. Overnight, my poultry profits died — along with more than 500 chickens. Where does one "put" hundreds of deceased chickens?

Do it *now.*

I shoveled all the stiff feathered fryers into my pickup truck and hauled them to the Ashby Land Fill, where a fire smoldered continuously, a murky likeness of the netherworld.

No one was around, so I piled my poultry into a smoking pit, satisfied that they would magically turn to ashes in a few hours. The heavy odor of burning feathers reassured me as I drove away.

The Ashby town meeting that week happened to be much less boring than usual. I sat toward the back of the room, and a man, whose face was as red as a rooster comb, led the discussion.

"Rotten! Stinking! Someone had the nerve to throw *thousands* of chickens in the dump! Of course, the chicken flesh didn't burn! They're still there, rotting away ..."

The Ashby flock inside the town hall was growing more agitated, and I resisted an urge to correct the man — only a few *hundred* of my fryers died. I suddenly remembered an important appointment, and it was the last town meeting I attended for quite some time.

I phased out poultry farming.

ॐॐॐ

Art's Photo, City Plate Co., Firestone Tire, Portsmouth Motel, warehouses, banks, shopping centers, nursing homes, manufacturing and industrial buildings — all these jobs, based

The best is yet to come

upon our reputation, ran through our new office on an 8-acre parcel we bought from Leonard Somero.

But we never lost sight of who we were just a few years before: carpenters with big families and big mortgages. Seppala & Aho Construction Company had become successful, but our offices reflected humility. We built the offices like a house, easily remodeled and sold as a single-family home if we failed in our grandiose ventures.

Architects often challenged us with mountains that seemed impossible to move, like excavating a massive dump site to find bedrock before constructing commercial buildings. Many times in the bidding process, God gave us favor over other companies, even when our presentation lacked the sophistication of "big business."

We had just demolished a building for a Jewish group at Fitchburg, with debris laying in helter-skelter piles, when I escorted investors around their building site. In my trademark buoyant style, I constructed a beautiful synagogue for their imaginations, until I tripped backward and sat heavily upon a board with a long rusty nail. I didn't *sit* there for very long, but threw back a hand to shove myself up and off the projectile … and jammed another nail into my palm, almost clean through.

I ended up at the doctor's office for a tetanus shot and bandages. But we built their synagogue, with an eternal light glowing and a sacred room for the Torah.

I usually took the lead in projects that no one else could accomplish or that no one else was foolish enough to try. While building a motel in Portsmouth, New Hampshire, our crane operator swung his boom too far and hit a ball on top of a 50-foot flag pole. The slender rod attaching the ball to the pole had bent over, a cinch to fix, if it were within reach.

"Hoist me up!" I wrapped my legs around the cable and gave the crane operator the thumbs up. He hesitated, but the *boss* was signaling. He hit the lever.

Endings and beginnings

Fifty feet seemed like a mile as I swung back and forth like a wrecking ball. I held onto the cable so hard that my fingers nearly indented the steel! No way could I budge that rod, the rod that looked so "flimsy" from the ground. My men enjoyed watching me swing and, even more, my colorless face that couldn't hide relief when I was on terra firma. A good joke relieved our men of the frustrations at being away from family for weeks at a time in our portable camps.

Business wasn't the only project in my life that was expanding. Two more children were born while we lived at our little home on Richardson Road, and Barbara was pregnant again. With seven on the ground and one on the way, we needed *room*. Semmi sold us 12 acres right across the road from our house on Richardson, and I set men to building our new gambrel-roof home with a giant-sized living room, spacious kitchen and dining room. Upstairs we all slept in four large bedrooms, and below the house we dug a basement for storage. Like our old house, we built a breezeway between the two-car garage and the house, with a crowning Finnish touch: our sauna.

The 10 of us moved into our dream home, and I got to work on a two-story addition at the rear of the house containing more bedrooms and, most importantly, another bathroom. Our basement turned out to be a perfect den for get-togethers, and Hjalmer and I had a grand idea. We painted the basement a cheerful green and dug a pit outside to broil dozens of broiler halves at one time. We invited all our men and their families to share a wonderful meal, and our first company barbecue was a smashing success. About 100 people came, and the barbecue became a yearly tradition for more than 30 years.

At this second house on Richardson Road, we seldom had an evening without guests. Our love of children, food and fun proved an open invitation to relatives (most with growing families) and friends who soaked up our Finnish culture and

The best is yet to come

hospitality. Saturday nights were reserved especially for "sauna company," and we sang or talked late into the evenings.

On weekends, I drove to Leominster and bought crates of bananas, strawberries and anything else fruity to mix as a fruit salad for guests. We had the biggest family in the neighborhood, and children from up and down the street came to "where the action was" — to eat from Marty's giant bowl of fruit.

Several folks from our church in New Ipswich lived nearby: the Lampinens, Korpis, Ojalas and Goddards. Each family held a special place in our hearts as we raised our children along with theirs for 14 wonderful years. In fact, we were blessed with nine more of our own at our Richardson Road ranch.

Our kids seldom passed a weekend without sleepover company. Saturday nights, the kids and their friends played late. But everyone knew that on Sunday, Marty required him or her to be out of bed for breakfast before services.

"Everybody up! Get ready for church. Breakfast!"

Most of the time, my kids heard me stomping up the stairs and hopped out of bed, ready to get dressed. But the uninitiated sleeping stragglers who snored over my booming voice ended up with a drizzle of water on their face to help them wake up.

Soon the herd gathered from every corner of the house to our big dining room table for morning prayer.

Pancakes, stacked on big platters, and mounds of Little Smokies embellished Barbara's table, and the kids ate all they could hold. Pitchers of orange juice made the rounds until empty, refilled and emptied again. At church, our big station wagon spilled out laughing, romping kids that gave our elderly folk a reason to smile … or frown.

Nearly a half century later, men with gray beards stop me on the street laughing and reminding me, not of Uncle Marty's great blueberry pancakes (which were my specialty for years), but of his "water treatment" they experienced as a boy.

Endings and beginnings

Over the years, each son and daughter grew in their own fertile soil, essential to our Seppala legacy. This Family Poem was written by Barbara, for each of her special ones.

Now listen, my children, I've a story to tell,
And when it's all over, you'll say we've done well.
Your dad and I were married in the merry month of May,
And we really must admit, we had a happy wedding day.
Before the first year was over, our little Dan appeared,
The cutest little man, we thought, that God had ever made.
Next came Sandy, the sweetest little miss,
Her daddy called her Dolly, she was his joy and bliss.
Now along came Annie, she was such a quiet girl,
And how we marveled when her hair began to curl.
Wow, then came little Sambo; Dad was very, very proud,
He blew the horn from Winchendon to Ashby clear and loud.
My, how could we be so lucky to have Debbie come along,
She always cleaned the house with a happy, happy song.
Out of nowhere our Jonathan did appear,
All that we could think of was a spunky Teddy Bear.
Next came Wanda, the "Maiden of Love,"
We really were so lucky to have her come from above.
Our Joel was the next one, my, oh my, he was sweet,
He never got into the way of anybody's feet.
Then came little Nathan, another quiet boy,
He really only had his thumb for a toy.
Benjamin was the next one who did from God appear,
We shouted "Hallelujah — no more please, Savior dear."
But our Lord, he didn't listen; he had other things in store.
We really didn't mean it when we said, "A dozen more!"
When Matthew came along, we already had ten,
Could Mother manage another in her pen?
My, oh my, we were happy when Heidi came along,
She really is a joy to us when she plays a lovely song.

The best is yet to come

Next came Jason Amos, or so your mother said,
Till your dad changed it to Amos Jason instead.
Then came Joshua, who was born with a smile,
He really didn't realize we had come a long, long mile.
Now along came little Mindy with the sparkling, eager eyes,
She thinks that to her parents she had no apron ties.
Then came our Marci, with a sweet word of cheer,
To anyone who will bend a listening ear.
Our Millie is the grand finale,
And here it is, my tale to tell.

Chapter five
Seasons of destiny

Jesus has been master of my vineyard for fourscore and more, and I comprehend his designs in ways that young Martin Seppala never could. Today, I identify with the host at the marriage feast at Cana, who tasted Jesus' miracle wine toward the *end* of the festivities.

He exclaimed, "Thou hast kept the good wine until now!" (John 2:10).

Family.

Every chore, every supper together and every mishap or delight that Barbara and I experienced with our children sent moral tendrils deeper into their souls. In our family, incidents and accidents have never been "coincidence." God's eternal purposes (unseen and unspoken at the time) have been appreciated *later.*

A guardian angel drove Bill Korpi's big red convertible one Sunday afternoon.

Several dozen kids, toddlers to teens, ran up and down our stairs and across our lawn after church. Bill had backed into the driveway, parking in front of the garage. The concrete driveway sloped away from our house. The inviting gearshift, pedals and white leather seats awakened the future driver in every red-blooded boy and girl playing nearby. Ten kids piled into Bill's Pontiac to take it for a "pretend" spin.

Screams upset our sermon discussions indoors. We burst outside just in time to watch Bill's Pontiac gaining speed toward a stone wall, kids bailing out along the way. The remaining passengers kept yowling until the car crumpled its front bumper as it climbed the wall to perch high-centered. Each father grabbed his kids from the pretty white seats to check for broken bones, then thoroughly scolded each one when we knew they were okay. Bill stood with his hands on his head, staring at his prize, which had acquired an extreme overbite.

"Mom! Fire truck's coming!" Barbara didn't hear any siren, but there was something in Joey's tone that made her stop ironing and go outside to stand on the porch.

Suddenly an engine wailed past our house and swung into Eino Ojala's driveway.

"What's going on, Joey?"

Our 8 year old's eyes grew wide as saucers as he confessed. "Bobby Ojala and me were building a *teeny* fire out of twigs and pine needles." He looked down, reliving the terror. "We got a pail of water from a barrel out behind the house to put the fire out, but it blew up and got bigger!"

The boys had "extinguished" their teeny fire with kerosene.

I always wondered what happened to the plastic pails we used for soaping and washing up inside our sauna. Nobody seemed to know anything about it when I asked, and I had to buy new pails. Years later, the truth came out.

Nate, our ninth child, had been experimenting to see how hot he could get the sauna, using dry hardwood ends that I hauled home from General Box in Winchendon. Only God's grace prevented the sauna from burning down. The buckets had melted into greasy plastic heaps, and after they cooled, the boys tossed them into the woods to hide the evidence.

Nate loved his little dog. We bought him a pup, and he cared for it himself one winter. Nate thought that giving the pup a bath would make Mom happy, so he scrubbed the dog and put him outside to dry. The temperature was below zero.

Seasons of destiny

Mom and Dad came home from shopping, and Nate's dog stood waiting to get inside, clean, but frozen *stiff.*

The day our 13th child, Amos, was born, I barely made it to my meeting with the owner of McAlister Manufacturing. The session was to finalize a contract, and bankers, owners and attorneys sat impatiently at a big oval table as I burst into the room, wearing my customary "baby" grin. A disturbing chill hung in the room as I took a chair, as though I had been the subject of conversation.

Mr. McAlister fixed me with a cynical gaze. "Is it true that this is your *13th* child?"

"Yes, sir!" I said, smiling around the table at the incredulous professionals.

"Not so smart of you to have so many children, Seppala." I detected a hopeless strain in his voice.

"You know," I said, "the way things are going in this world, it may not be smart. But when I consider life in the light of eternity, it's another story."

McAlister looked thoughtful for a moment. "Well, I guess that shuts my mouth," he said and nodded at his paperwork. The room suddenly warmed up.

I only saw McAlister's own son once. Then I understood his sentiments. Twisted by muscular dystrophy, his boy painfully struggled to walk with his father across a worksite. I realized that McAlister labored harder in caring for just one child than I did for my whole big family.

How our home survived 17 children without burning to a crisp could only have been through God's grace alone. Amos and Joshua played with a cigarette lighter in their bedroom, but got no flaming satisfaction until they found matches in the kitchen. After striking a bunch and tossing each one under their mattress, the ticking finally began to ignite. Nate, who was supposedly babysitting while Mom and Dad were out, smelled smoke.

Amos and Joshua weren't about to face their older brother *and* Dad. So they figured on locking out the world outside their room. They pushed furniture against the door, while Nate screamed warnings and threats.

The little guys finally got so scared, however, of the smoke filling the room that they finally let Nate inside. He doused the mattress with a bucket of water, then hauled the smoldering mattress outside.

When I came home that night, I heard the story. The mattress wasn't even smoldering anymore, so I left it until the next day.

But by morning the mattress had "branded" our lawn, and only an outline of ashes remained. Evidently latent embers had burrowed deep and hot inside and burned up the whole mattress during the night.

One Sunday, my legs turned to jelly when Heidi screamed, "Mindy's fallen out of the upstairs window!"

I pictured the concrete patio below the back window two stories down. There was nothing to break her fall. But our 2 year old had leaned too far out the *front* upper story window, below which thick shrubs were planted. She had fallen on the shrubs and barely had a scratch.

Mindy was our 15th child, and like my other kids, she loved to help her daddy. In the evening when I got home from work, I would kick off my shoes and recline in the La-Z-Boy.

"How about a drink?" I would ask, and if Mindy was handy, off she would toddle to Mom, who gave her a cup of cold water to carry to Dad.

She concentrated on *me* all the way across the living room, proud and smiling with a grimy little hand clasped over the top of the cup to keep the water inside. It sloshed between her dirty fingers, and as she handed it to me, she watched carefully as I drank every drop.

It was her desire to please her daddy. She expected him to accept what she offered without reservation.

This is so like our relationship with our Heavenly Father: We want to please him, but all our good works are tainted with so much grime — unclean thoughts, anger, fleshly desires. But God accepts us without reservation because of Jesus' precious blood.

A child really knows a father's heart. Marci, our 16th child, told me that a girlfriend's dad wanted to buy some equipment I left in an old warehouse. Marci asked me if I would sell it to him. I told her to tell her girlfriend that her dad was welcome to take it away, free of charge.

"Dad, I knew you'd say that!" She looked proudly at me. "I already told my friend that her dad could *have* it and that you didn't want any money!"

My little girl knew me well enough to speak for me. Do I know God's heart well enough that I can confidently speak of his will to others?

The Seppalas' nine shaggy boys should have been our local barber's dream come true. But I bought my *own* barber chair at an auction. I hauled it home and installed it in the basement next to the laundry chute (the kids used this chute instead of stairs). I bought scissors, combs and clippers and could have fashioned every cut known to barber-dom. But I learned only two styles instead: butch and flattop.

Neighbor boys often lined up with my own sons for cuts, and I never had time to contact their mothers for permission. I just sheared them and shooed them out. I never heard a complaint. But as the boys turned 15 years old, they quit coming, including my own sons.

The best is yet to come

The Seppala fashion had suddenly dropped out of vogue.

On summer Sunday afternoons, Barbara often packed a picnic lunch for the family, and we crammed into the station wagon with towels and toys for a swim at Hubbard Pond. I knew about a secret swimming hole down a narrow gravel road rarely used.

Our kids still talk about the bumpy ride, rather than swimming. At the top of the turnoff, I would park for a moment. I can still hear the joyful squeals when I let down the tailgate on the station wagon. As many as could fit would perch on the tailgate. Then I chugged along the rutty old road, peering through the rearview mirror as my boys and girls hopped on and off all the way to the swimming hole.

Engineering the simplest fun activity for my kids germinated and grew into wonderful memories for them. All it took was a little creativity and patience on my part.

These days I encounter my Heavenly Father as I ruminate about my 17 children. Each child has enriched my spiritual life. Precious is God's intervention in our varied lives, and I treasure every blessed recollection.

ॐ॰ॐ॰ॐ

Dreaming of and creating my own commercial enterprise grated against a collective force on the East Coast that scorned individualism. I unknowingly challenged this force by simply giving men and women good jobs. Trade unions met my challenge with belligerent picketers, carrying signs and sometimes weapons.

For us to survive and expand, Seppala & Aho Construction Company, now based in New Ipswich, searched out tradesmen who also refused to cower under union threats. Our wages and care of individual workers reflected our Christian ideals, a foreign concept in most business environments. Our paradigm attracted excellent employees and superintendents.

We chose as leaders within S&A experts in the trades that needed to complete the dozens of commercial jobs pouring into our office: plumbing, electrical, sprinkler systems, roofing, carpentry, masonry, laborers, painting and drywall, steel fabricators and steel erectors. We also tapped the best architects we could find to design our structures. Many of our employees were Christians that we knew from our Apostolic Lutheran faith and other churches as well.

In time, we handled all phases of our customers' needs, including assisting in furnishing their mall, home or high-rise. Our workforce grew in experience and sheer manpower, stomping the toes of nearly every trade union on the East Coast.

Our first large acquisition was the Minuteman Redimix Concrete plant in Leominster, Massachusetts. Mike Olson, my sister Elaine's husband, was my partner in the purchase, and we were able to circumvent the union shops that refused to cross picket lines and fill our concrete forms. As we grew, we filled the crosshairs of union organizers who expected us to kowtow to their authority.

While we broke ground for a shopping center at Matheun, Massachusetts, the unions gathered forces at our construction gate entrance. We shipped concrete 35 miles from our plant in Leominster which enraged and activated the unions' organizers. Their 100 picketers seemed to be handpicked for their foul language and creative, nasty signs.

For a while, only verbal threats bombarded our trucks as they passed the gates and dumped their loads of concrete. But driving *out* of the jobsite was a different story. Picketers closed ranks in front of the trucks, and the drivers feared that they might mangle someone if they rolled on.

"Pull your air horn steady, and set the truck in low gear. They'll move!" Mike Olson told a driver when he called for instructions. Our driver blasted the air horn and moved forward, but the surly picketers stood their ground. The driver called Mike again.

"I'm on the way."

Mike hopped into the cement truck, jammed it into low gear and held the air horn as steady as his churning tires. His bumper connected with the first picketers, and they wisely backed away, slamming their signs on the hood. Three brave ones lay across the wide bumper as Mike gained speed away from the rabble.

It's going to be a cold ride clear to Leominster.

No sooner had Mike contemplated this, than the men jumped off, except one. He hopped off to the side and fell into a ditch. Mike never looked back. An ambulance arrived and collected the man, but not a word was said about any injury. No one tried to stop our trucks again at the Matheun Mall job.

But at our construction site in East Hartford, Massachusetts, we faced a more organized and violent opposition. We searched far and wide to secure open-shop tradesmen, hiring a Puerto Rican masonry subcontractor for the foundation work. Bud White ran the whole job for us as supervisor and kept us apprised of the progress daily, sometimes hourly.

The situation heated up a little at a time, like my sons' mattress smoldering on the lawn. Picketers swarmed and chanted curses as our men warily drove past them to work. It seemed to be a one-sided war of words (they were winning that battle!) until a truck loaded with sand rolled up to the gate. The picketers challenged the driver, and he stopped dead. Our Puerto Rican boss waved from a scaffold to the trucker to come through, finally jumping down to talk to him at his window.

The picketers couldn't wait to get to our mason. Suddenly he lay on the ground bleeding as the union thugs beat him with short pieces of chain. Our masons poured off their scaffolds, and the melee left picketers all over the ground, like battered bowling pins.

The masons had come prepared. They carried nunchucks (two nightsticks with a short chain linking them) in their big lunchboxes, standard equipment for non-union jobs. Our tough Puerto Rican masonry supervisor came back to the job the next day, laughing, his head bandaged up like a mummy.

But the union activists had plenty of resources to pull from, and they refused to leave.

"Martin, there are more picketers than ever. It's getting harder to get through the lines. Should I try to move 'em?" Bud White was a Marine and spoiling for a fight.

"No. I'll be there in the morning, Bud. I'll go through the line with you."

It was only right that the boss leave his office chair and face the danger with his men.

I recruited Wayne Kinnunen, my son Nate and Ralph Niemela, Jr. to join me.

We arrived early, and Bud White was already getting organized. "I let the cops know we're going into our jobsite today, Martin. I told them they needed to help us get through."

I followed Bud's lead. He drove his pickup, and I came second, in my brand-new Ford station wagon. Behind us were several workmen inside another car.

"Get as many pictures of the whole mess as you can," I instructed Wayne and Ralph, handing them cameras.

"Good night!" someone said as we turned the corner into a sea of picketers who couldn't wait to swarm the vehicles, screaming. We slowly proceeded down the narrow gravel road until union men plugged the entrance to our jobsite as tight as a bung in a barrel.

Police officers mingled with the crowd of 400 or more, trying to push back the picketers.

"Keep the dirty scabs out!"

The best is yet to come

A red-faced man with a scuffed-up bullhorn screamed scratchy epithets, egging on the herd.

"These d*** Canucks from Canada are stealing food from your babies' mouths!"

Swearing. Threats. Bedlam.

A police car eased into the riot, and an officer stood at his car door with a mic to his lips: "These men are legally going into their worksite right now. Make way!"

Officers pushed back the crowd and waved us into a widening gap of signs, torsos, arms and legs. We drove slowly, hoping no one fell under the tires. Bud's pickup swayed side-to-side as if waves beat from both directions, and we could see the cause: the picketers' boots kicking the doors on both sides. Tools disappeared as union men looted the truck bed. The truck's aerial was snapped off, and a hoodlum swung it against the cab over and over.

Suddenly a loud report quieted the mob, but it wasn't gunfire. We realized that one of Bud's tires had been knifed. Another report, and no one blinked. Now Bud's truck limped on two aired-up front tires through the gate. Picketers suddenly closed the gap in our wretched parade, standing in front of my station wagon. Police screamed at them to clear the way as picket signs slammed against the car hood. The officers physically grabbed men and shoved them aside as we moved through.

My Ford rocked back and forth, and I briefly recalled the hurricane of '38. Then I heard the *bang!* My car jolted lower, and I knew someone had stabbed one of my tires, too. The ocean grew rougher for a moment before we passed into safe harbor: the private property beyond the gate.

I stopped the car and got out, watching the last car, with four flats hobble toward us, jubilant picketers throwing debris after them.

"Well, at least we got lots of photographs."

"Uh, Marty. I got a few …" Ralph said, but Wayne looked embarrassed.

"I *forgot* to take any in all that confusion."

I took stock of the situation and decided, "We can't stay here today, fellas. We'll shut down. When the cops leave there's no telling what the union boys'll try to do. We can't work with one eye on them all day."

My car was the most easily repaired for driving, so after a tire change we piled into the station wagon and left the job by another route. I called our attorneys, then met them at the courthouse in East Hartford.

The heads of the trade unions were there as well. They had something to tell me.

"Mr. Seppala, as of today, all picket lines will be taken away, and we will not picket at the site again."

Our attorneys filled us in: "It's illegal for the union to threaten or impede the owner of a construction company in reaching his worksite. You won this round."

To look at our vehicles, no one else would have thought so.

Of all the union harassment we experienced over the decades, the strangest occurred in Providence, Rhode Island, once a headquarters for East Coast organized crime. We *expected* trade unions to picket us when we broke ground for a shopping center in Providence, because it was situated so close to its governing mafia authority.

We immediately hired a guard service to watch over equipment and structures at the jobsite. They circulated among our employees and got wind of a union plot to knock down the steel framework we had erected.

One morning, as they arrived to work, our men passed a battered car at the gate. The car's windshield had been shot out, as well as the headlights. The security guard called me with the story. At the midnight shift change, three guards were sitting in our job trailer when a suspicious car pulled up, blinking its headlights and honking. One of the guards drew his weapon and approached the car. The other two headed off to discover what the clanking noises were near the newly built steel structures.

Someone in the union thug's car fired a pistol at the approaching guard, and he flattened out on the ground, firing from the prone position until the car headlights were blown out. The other two guards fired into the air to scare away the thugs trying to ruin our steel. The culprits escaped, and fortunately no one was killed.

According to some pretty reliable sources, the union organizers wanted me dead, and I had some strange thoughts as I sat near our picture window in the evening.

Not long after the shooting at the jobsite, a man named Nate Gregory called to tell me he had "good news."

"I really need to talk with you in person, Mr. Seppala," he said. I agreed to meet with him at his chosen location, the junction of highways 495 and 119.

"I'll be there, but I won't be alone," I told him.

He laughed a little and said, "You bring whoever you want."

It wasn't hard to select my bodyguard.

"I'm meeting with the mafia today. Can you come along?" I asked Bob Hakala, the most fearless man I knew and a guy who loved excitement.

We parked at the quiet intersection near a big black Caddy, and a man rolled down his window.

"Get in, so we can talk, Seppala." Bob and I both took a seat, warily.

"Martin, I've got good news for you: I can get rid of the dogs on your tail at the Providence jobsite, and it won't cost you much at all!"

Mr. Gregory seemed to think he was doing me a great favor as he continued. "To get rid of the dogs, I've got to pay off the guys higher up, you know."

Seasons of destiny

He lit up a cigarette and puffed a cloud of smoke out the window.

"It'll cost $5,000 bucks for me to pull it off."

Bob Hakala sat expressionless. I stared at the little dark-haired man in an expensive suit and said, "That's pretty cheap to get the unions off my back …"

He smiled wide, nodding, like he had just sunk an eight ball.

"But my conscience would never let me do that."

His smile disappeared, and so did any friendliness in his voice. "That's okay, Martin. Then we'll just keep fighting …"

Bob and I got out of the car, and I never saw Mr. Gregory again, but I felt repercussions from our meeting not long after.

One morning when Mike Olson arrived at our Minuteman Redimix Concrete plant, he called me with bad news.

"Martin, someone dynamited the place last night."

"How bad, Mike?"

"Bad. The steel walls are blown out. The equipment seems to be intact, though. Just another day at the office, I guess."

Mike's truck drivers had been complaining about union men crowding their trucks off the highway as they tried to deliver loads. But Mike never gave in to discouragement.

We were forced to shut down the concrete plant for weeks, and the business community around Leominster was outraged over the open violence used by the trade union. Even Keating Concrete called us and said they were mad as h*** and offered to batch all our trucks to finish up jobs.

When we could afford it, Mike and I decided to build another concrete batch plant in Nashua with better security. We moved the whole kit and caboodle to that location and stayed there until we sold the concrete company years later.

The best is yet to come

Simple comforts, uncommon loyalty.

After a long day of declining mafia bribes, dodging union thugs and nailing down multi-million-dollar projects, I couldn't wait to get home to my La-Z-Boy. In fact, I decided that all my hardworking employees deserved rocker-recliners as well. To reward their loyalty, I called the La-Z-Boy manufacturer and asked for a price on 200 chairs. We agreed upon a generous discount, and they sent a catalog. I chose a variety of styles and colors before they sent the armchairs by railcar to Rindge.

We warehoused them at our facility at New Ipswich, where we had our Christmas party. Each husband and wife picked out a La-Z-Boy for their living room or den.

Every year, Seppala & Aho doled out a variety of gifts to employees based upon years of service: new employees received gifts worth $200, three-to-five-year veterans received gifts valued at $300 and those serving five years or more were honored with gifts worth $500. After poring over catalogs, our workers claimed their rewards, and we delivered them to their homes by Christmas. I lost count of the thousands of La-Z-Boys we awarded over the decades we were in business.

At one time, we had around 600 employees, and presenting these gifts became a full-time job for one employee. Months in advance of the annual party, Bill Peterson planned the lengthy process of ordering, storing and assigning appreciation gifts.

Another annual event, the Seppala & Aho barbecue, had a distinctly Finnish flavor. We sprayed our "secret" formula of vinegar and saltwater on 800 chicken halves and tossed them onto racks in long open pits. The office help and company superintendents served our men and women, a gesture of gratitude to our employees and their wonderful families.

My Christian experience. My Family. My Business.

Keeping priorities in proper order as a businessman is like walking an I-beam during construction of a high-rise. God's mercy was my safety harness, and Jesus often arrested my plunge off cold steel.

Working shoulder-to-shoulder with Christian men and women has been as vital to my success as spanning my malls with engineered, quality girders. Their counsel and integrity helped me deal with decisions concerning personnel, finances, safety and expansion.

I was a young carpenter when God sorted through all the good men in my life and chose Hjalmer Aho as my first partner. How God welded together such utterly diverse grades of steel I'll never know!

While hanging over rafters, dimes and quarters pelted the subfloor beneath me, and I never bothered to pick them up. But Hjalmer hoarded his change in a little coin purse that he fed like a precious pet.

I guesstimated jobs. Hjalmer often rescued me from making decisions moved by my impatience. I chased down opportunities and wrestled them into submission. Hjalmer graciously enriched our dreams with his shrewd financial insight.

The scope of our achievements rang like a hammer on flatiron as we built families, businesses and strong relationships across the East Coast. To this day, my old friend holds a special place in my heart, and pleasant memories run free as I take stock of our exciting years.

I have employed scores of good people from the Apostolic Lutheran Church, of which I have been a member my whole life. It wasn't always comfortable for an unbeliever to work alongside so many dyed-in-the-wool Christians. It was rumored that anyone who cursed on our jobs would be fired, but this wasn't the case!

God changed hearts as tradesmen and laborers worked shoulder-to-shoulder with fine Christian men. I recall a beaming wife of one employee who said that her husband had stopped swearing altogether after months on the job with us.

We still believe that our workplace is our mission field, and our goal is to help prepare our neighbors for eternal life. Repentance and acceptance of Jesus as Savior is the only way to leave this world with the assurance of a home in heaven.

As men in the top tier of commercial enterprise in the nation, we were respected in our communities. Men troubled in their souls often came to us for advice or help.

"I never cry like this when I'm sober!" A bedraggled man who stumbled onto the job told me about his monumental struggle to master the demons of alcohol.

From wide-ranging vantage points, God positioned me to show men the true love of Jesus: from my corporate offices, from a pickup seat and sometimes in rubber boots shoveling concrete. How could I know that, at the pinnacle of my success, God was "roughing in" endurance to help me deal with unbearable loss? How could I know he would launch me into ministries I never imagined?

Martin Seppala's *Do it now* was being reshaped into *Do it in God's time.*

In the late 1960s and early 70s, relationships with wealthy investors grew more satisfying. In our dialogues, I didn't shrink from presenting to them the gospel message, hoping they would confess Jesus as Savior. My reputation as an honest entrepreneur spread like a system of anchoring roots in the upper East Coast. The usual whiskey or martinis never sullied our conferences, and sometimes it was what I refused to accept that blessed our company the most.

Transparency.

One day, Dave Olson met with a man to negotiate a lucrative construction project: a shopping center for a large company. We had pretty well closed the deal when the representative added one caveat. "Dave, I need $50,000 for helping you obtain this contract. I need it in cash, and you can add it to your bid, so that it won't cost your company a cent."

Dave never blinked. As a Christian man, he agreed with my conviction about bribes, kickbacks, payola and general under-the-table dealings. "I'm sorry, but we don't operate that way," he said. "We're transparent in all our company accounting. We'll be happy to pay you out in the open."

"H*** no! My payment must be in cash and under the table!" He grabbed up his blueprints and stomped out of our office.

Another day, I watched a profitable international opportunity evaporate before my eyes when a group of men offered me a momentous project in South Vietnam. The war had just ended, and companies were bidding on multi-million-dollar proposals to rebuild the ravaged nation.

"Mr. Seppala, we have thoroughly vetted your firm and believe that your company is best positioned to help us create infrastructure in South Vietnam. Are you interested?"

It was easy to answer that one.

"Then we'll be in touch." We shook hands around the table, and the Asian business magnates left our humble office.

A few days passed, then they called to ask for a second meeting. "You have been awarded the first of several contracts that will be issued. This first one should top about 300 million dollars."

"I do have some questions," I said. "What if war breaks out again before we complete the contract?"

"The South Vietnamese government will provide assurances that you will come away with substantial earnings in the event that work is halted."

Could this contract get any sweeter?

"We do have one, ah, *wrinkle*, to be ironed out," the spokesman continued. "A few renegade warlords live in the mountains where you'll be constructing warehouses.

Substantial costs to appease these military leaders should be included in the final bid."

"Warlords?"

"Yes, Mr. Seppala."

I wondered if I was staring into the eyes of one of these "warlords" as I said, "To bribe anyone is something that my conscience will not allow, sir. I'm sorry."

"Oh, I hope you will reconsider. This is a very routine procedure in Asian countries. We call it 'commission' rather than the crass term, 'bribe.'"

"I'm not going to *bribe* anyone," I replied, and my Finnish hackles began to bristle.

The men about the table all stood up, and one man nearly shouted, "You'll never see another deal as profitable as this one, Mr. Seppala! Never! The paperwork is ready to be signed. It's all ready to go!"

"I don't doubt that," I said, opening the door. "I cannot in good conscience deal with you."

We never heard from these men again.

Standing upon principle seemed counterproductive, but God rewarded our honesty by sending a message throughout the industry that Seppala & Aho could be trusted.

Sam Tamposi and Gerry Nash worked with me for more than 30 years, and most of our massive projects were begun with a simple handshake. Sam and Gerry became the largest commercial developers in New Hampshire, and we became the largest contractor in the state. Seppala & Aho constructed more than 100 malls, high-rises, warehouses and other commercial buildings for these men, often with several projects rolling at the same time.

"Martin, I have a customer who wants an industrial building ..."

Sam would project overall measurements, and we would estimate the price for designing and building the structure, from grading to completion. By the end of the day, he would decide how to cover all costs and profit by leasing the buildings. We both wrote down our figures, and Gerry would finalize the job. I drew funds from their account each month during the construction process.

At the completion of the project, we would figure cost overruns, and I don't recall a single disagreement over the years. We designed and built several car dealerships for Sam and Gerry: showrooms, garages and service areas for Ford, Chevrolet, Buick, Dodge, Volkswagen, Lincoln and Cadillac.

The grandest venture we landed with my two friends was through Sanders Associates: construction of two defense industrial buildings for top-secret research and manufacturing. In a joint venture with Sam and Gerry, we worked through a freezing winter to erect structures with special bulwarks in the ceilings and roofs to prevent security breaches. In the 1970s, a contract for $20 million was a lot of money.

In the midst of my dreams of expansion, God often reminded me that I needed to be connected to the young people in my community. I accepted the responsibility to do what I could to help boys and girls grow into honest, reliable leaders. Many fine adults had contributed to my future. Frank Martin, so patient as I trailed behind him and his draft horses. Uncle Bill, a Godly example of manhood. Miss Youngquest, who challenged me to learn. Mr. White, my Boy Scout leader. Pastor Anderson, who led me to a deeper walk with Jesus. My beloved mother, whose fearless preaching I emulated. And my father, whose strong influence still shapes my every decision.

The successes I experienced afforded me opportunities that most could only dream of. One year the company purchased toolboxes filled with tools for our employees. We warehoused the 100 shiny red boxes for our annual Christmas party. But the next day, I received a phone call from a distraught employee.

The best is yet to come

"Every toolbox is gone! Someone jimmied the lock and stole every single one of them!"

I called the police, then drove directly to the warehouse to meet them there. The officers were outraged at the brazenness of the theft. As I watched them take fingerprints, I told them that the stolen items were Christmas presents for our working families. After they finished, I relocked the doors to the empty warehouse.

A week passed, and nothing surfaced. So my impatience set me on a tear. "Barbara, I'm not waiting anymore. I'm going to find that thief myself!"

It must have been bugging Barbara, too. "I'm going with you," she said. So we trolled from gas station to gas station making inquiries, hoping someone had tried to sell the tools to a repair shop.

The next day we got a good solid lead. The name Dickie Carlton floated to the surface. According to my source, he knew who had stolen the tools.

I couldn't wait to talk to Dickie.

"You are in deep trouble, son," I pronounced over the phone. "You stole my toolboxes, and I'm going to press charges. YOU are going to jail!"

I heard the panic in his voice as he blurted out, "I didn't do it! But I know who did!"

"I'm on the way over to your house, and when you see my headlights in your driveway, you get right out there to talk to me, and I won't tell your mom and dad."

He did exactly as he was told, and as he sat in my car, he named a local boy, Karl Johnson, as the one who had stolen the boxes. Karl had an accomplice who lived in Greenville, and they had dumped the tools in burlap bags and stored them in Karl's father's garage, then sunk the empty toolboxes in a lake.

My next stop after Dickie's was at a respectable home nearby, owned by Karl Johnson's folks. Karl's mom came to the door with a smile, until I announced loudly, "I need to speak to your son, right now."

Karl was a heavyset youth with arms that looked like he could shovel piles of gravel all day. I spoke to him at the door, loudly enough for his mother to hear. "You are the thief who stole 100 toolboxes from my company."

Karl turned to the kitchen behind him where his mother stood with folded arms.

"Mom! I don't know what this guy's talkin' about!" His face looked stricken. He called everyone who dared sully his reputation "liars" as I explained in detail exactly how he had taken the toolboxes and where the tools were stashed.

"Look, son. I'm going home. If you are ready to confess, I'll not press charges. I'll give you until 7:00 this evening to come by my house in Ashby. If you miss the appointment, you're going to jail. We even have your fingerprints at the warehouse."

At home I read the newspaper in my La-Z-Boy, waiting.

"We have company, Marty," Barbara said, and Mindy joined her at the window. Headlights shone past the curtains and I headed out the door. It was a little before 7:00.

The defensive, belligerent Karl had stayed at home. The boy who appeared at my door, with slumping shoulders and tear-stained cheeks, owned up to his crime completely. And it didn't end with bringing back the tools he had stolen. A few days later, Karl confessed to other thefts, not to the authorities, but to me.

"I still have the stuff, and ... could you go with me when I give it all back?"

The next day after work I backed up my pickup to his dad's garage and helped Karl load up a nice set of acetylene tanks and brass torches. Then an outboard boat motor. As we pulled up to the scene of his boat motor theft, I stood by him while he knocked on the door.

"This boy has a confession to make to you, sir."

Karl laid open the events and hung his head, but the man

shook his vigorously. "Why did you bring that d*** thing back? I collected full payment from my insurance company. What am I going to do now?"

We set the motor in the same spot from which Karl had stolen it and left.

Our next stop: the place where Karl stole the torch set.

"I have to believe that there's a God after all," the offended little man said, pointing at the sky. "I never thought I'd see my tanks and torch again!"

Karl was quiet as we drove away.

"Anything else?" I asked.

"Yes, sir. I stole money from the register at the gas station when the owner wasn't looking."

I turned the car around.

When Karl confessed to the gas station owner and handed him the amount he had stolen, the man's reaction slapped both of us in our faces.

He snickered, "Why in the world would you bring this back? I never even knew it was gone."

I marveled at the lack of moral support or encouragement this boy received from two of the three adult figures he had wronged. In the course of their lives, how many young people would these men steer toward deceit and dishonesty?

I lost track of Karl after the events of that cold week at Christmastime. Later I heard that he had been murdered in Texas, and I'll always wonder about his eternal destination.

In the aftermath of my peculiar contact with Karl, an unusual awakening among other young men unsettled the youth in our community. Word spread about the mercy shown to Karl who took his medicine and openly confessed to his offenses. Other guilt-ridden young men came to *me*, and I pointed them to Jesus.

Their confessions varied: embezzling money from employers, experimenting with drugs, drinking communion

Seasons of destiny

wine at church, stealing collection money. Some of these boys are grown and wonderful Christian men with families of their own today.

An example: A couple of boys had stolen a Corvette at Franklin Pierce College. As in all cases, I maintained that restitution was an important part of confession and forgiveness. The Corvette owner had already received insurance money to replace the car. But sadly, the man had used the stolen car as an opportunity to profit. He told the police that a load of expensive musical instruments had been inside the trunk as well.

The boys had to pay for these phantom instruments, too. The detectives helping me deal with the issue of restitution told me that the Corvette owner ended up being a bigger crook than the young car thieves.

This community revival had a profound impact upon me, perhaps greater than upon those extraordinary young men who confessed to their crimes. I understood why my mother seldom let a visitor leave her hospitable home without asking if they were certain about their eternal destiny. An unquenchable thirst grew in my soul for others to receive forgiveness in the name and precious reconciling blood of Jesus.

My blessed mother passed away in 1963, two days before Barbara and I arrived in Ithaca, New York, to attend services at an Apostolic Lutheran Church. Mom suffered from diabetes, but her spirits were high and eyes bright as she anticipated a wonderful week together with Finnish families. After 14 years living as a widow, she had finally remarried a good man, Pa Impola, whom we all loved. My younger brother Arnold and his wife had driven Mom and Pa Impola to Ithaca and helped get them situated.

While staying with friends, Mom awoke and had spoken clearly in Finnish, "Now my hour of departure has come ..."

Arnold came to the room, and my mother lay back upon her pillow and closed her eyes.

The best is yet to come

"I am so tired," she said and gently slipped into the strong arms of Jesus.

Throughout her fruitful life, Mom was always certain of *where* she would spend eternity. Her legacy endures in the people she impacted over threescore and five years, and her ministry lives on through her boy with one cloudy eye.

He sees clearly that her destiny is his: to bring family and friends to a saving knowledge of Jesus Christ, then find peace in eternity where she waits to welcome him home.

Chapter six
Ascension at finn hill

Trust is valued higher among some men and women than all their wealth and resources.

After constructing a fast-food restaurant for the owner of a supermarket complex in Fitchburg, the man approached me about taking on more work.

It wasn't the conventional practice for Seppala & Aho to proceed without an investor's skin in the game, but this time I felt God's nudge and decided to trust Mike Demoulas.

And this multi-millionaire trusted me.

"Go ahead and start the job, Marty. Here are the blueprints. I'll get you a check."

After those first projects, 30 years ago, Mike and I built dozens of shopping centers and warehouses together, and I can't recall ever signing a single contract before shooting a grade.

Our personal connection surpassed clauses and fine print. Often Mike called me to his office to discuss a new idea, and over time, my concern for his eternal life touched him.

"Marty, look at me. Do you know of a time I cheated or hurt anyone?"

"Mike, I've heard nothing but good things about you. As for me, you've treated me better than anyone I've ever done business with."

Mike smiled at this. "Then what do I have to repent of?"

This opened a door to his heart, and I said, "The Bible tells us that every man is corrupted by sin. It's planted inside his very nature at birth — even in the very *best* of men."

I had to leave for a meeting, and I rose. "If you took all your thoughts for one day and wrote them on a billboard for all the world to see, how would you feel?"

"My God, Marty, that would be a catastrophe!"

"We *all* need a Savior, Mike," I said.

My hometown of Rindge, New Hampshire, always held a special place in my heart, and I explored the potential for a successful shopping center there. The closest Demoulas shopping plaza was 20 miles away in Fitchburg. So I decided to buy a patch of forested land along the new Highway 202. I did my due diligence in assessing demographics and costs, then proposed a plan for a new shopping center for Mike to consider.

"Marty, there's not a house within a quarter mile of this site! Why would people come from the neighboring towns to shop here in the *woods*?"

"I built my first chicken coop for a preacher here, Mike. I know these people. This mall will put Rindge on the map. A shopping center will draw other developers to build here, too. I tell you, this is a moneymaker!"

"Well, if this location ends up a flop, I'll erect a sign in your honor telling the world, 'Marty Seppala chose this site!'"

We had a good laugh, but I admit to having my own misgivings as we rolled out the construction in phases. Though the shopping center would expand Rindge's tax base and the town's residents would benefit from employment opportunities, the shortsighted town bureaucrats delayed our progress at every turn. They exacted more permits from us than any big city where we built shopping centers.

But after so many successful Seppala-Demoulas ventures, Mike trusted my judgment. Following church services on the day of our grand opening, some Seppala & Aho folks drove over to meet Mike and his wife at our new shopping plaza. Scores of cars filled the parking lot. To say the least, we were all relieved and overjoyed to be so blessed.

"Marty, I have a couple ideas to run past you. Can you spare an hour?"

I dropped by Mike's office, where he rolled out blueprints for an $8 million shopping center. My friend said, "It's yours, Marty."

He reached into his desk and hauled out another set of plans, a little smaller roll. "This one's only about $5 million. It's yours, too."

"How soon do you need me to start, Mike?" I asked, flummoxed at the suddenness of the back-to-back projects.

"Right now. I have a lot of cash kicking around. I bet you can use it better than I can. Why don't I give you an initial down payment?"

Mike handed me a check for $2 million.

"I'll give you a deposit on the smaller job, too."

I left his office with two rolls of prints, $3 million and not a lawyer in sight. We shook hands, with nothing signed.

But in all our years working together, our most meaningful encounter involved a blueprint of the most consequential enterprise of all. After chest pains and an ambulance ride to the hospital from his Florida seaside condominium, Mike Demoulas began mulling over the future, when he would leave behind all his bank accounts and land holdings.

We walked on the beach together and discussed religion and eternity, but I could sense the age-old question rising from his heart: "What must I do to be saved?" The gentle lap of ocean surf seemed the perfect music for words I know God placed in my mind.

"We've done a lot of business together, and we've always trusted one another," I said.

"Here's what I believe, Mike. In the Bible, Jesus said that he is the only way to the Father when this life ends. God's Son came to earth as a man and paid the penalty for our sin with his death on a cross so that we can have eternal life. Since he is

The best is yet to come

God, he rose from the dead. When we take him at his word and place our trust in his blood as payment for our sin, he confirms that we are saved by placing his Spirit in us. It's the contract that seals the deal."

Mike never jumped into decisions, and I left him to appraise God's compassionate invitation for his eternal investment.

While I aggressively shaped one of the largest contracting firms in the nation, a grievous event was about to reroute my future. I conducted business, completely unaware that my enterprising existence would take an unexpected turn. Mike Demoulas would have another opportunity to ponder the reality of life after death. Heartbreak and rejoicing would characterize the memorial service for my dear wife at our Apostolic Lutheran Church at New Ipswich.

ﾠﾠﾠﾠﾠﾠﾠﾠﾠﾠ๑๑๑๑

I had to convince Barbara how wonderful it would be to move away from Ashby (where she had lived her whole life) to Rindge, my old hometown.

"What about Mumu (Mother)? Who's going to comb her hair every Sunday?"

I rolled my eyes. Mumu and Semmi lived near our home in Ashby, and Barbara helped them with household tasks. It was one of our Sunday rituals for Mumu to call, a short time before we left for Sunday school. Barbara would "abandon" me to comb Mumu's hair, while I rifled through drawers and hampers to match up socks for 13 children!

I finally convinced Barbara to leave Ashby by promising her a beautiful new home. We hauled our Sunday rituals with us to a place we named Wind Swept Acres, and I built a cottage for Semmi and Mumu right next door to our house.

Ascension at finn hill

The new location grew on Barbara over time. The children loved our new haven, the taxes were lower and I could indulge in farming, a dream I had barely explored. And now Semmi and Mumu were even closer to us than at Ashby, and they loved their bungalow. Barbara settled into the life of a Finnish "farmer's" wife.

Our 120 acres had been part of a land holding established in 1776 called the French Farm. On it I constructed an eight-bedroom home to Barbara's specs, with two fireplaces, spacious kitchen, living room, den and sauna. To keep the feel of old New Hampshire, I built a colonial-style four-stall carriage shed and two-story barn, with a basketball court upstairs for the kids.

As the patriarch Finn farmer, I planned to parcel out Wind Swept Acres to sons and daughters someday. I had visions of all of us living close to one another, Barbara and I dandling grandchildren on our laps, surveying our holdings.

I never considered how free-spirited my offspring were. Like me. Winds of opportunity swept them from coast to coast!

My teenage children were ripe for farm work, and a scheme unfolded in my mind: I could keep them out of trouble with weeding, shoveling manure and tending livestock. That approach had certainly worked for my father. We planted a huge strawberry field and a nostalgic blueberry pasture. We fenced 40 acres and ran beef cattle through my handcrafted pole gate. The start of my growing herd was 10 heifers and a bull, plus there were horses for the children to ride.

Millet for cow feed, plenty of hard work, pickups loaded with grain sacks and neighbors rolling in and out all day — our farm barely slept. I spent my free time mending fences, feeding stock and ramrodding kids, which seemed harder than running picket lines and managing construction projects!

Barbara fed our farmhands and managed the household with a natural genius. At the end of each long day, her organ music expressed our hope for a wonderful morrow. My wife

The best is yet to come

humored me in my ranching ambitions as I expected that our investments would actually break even someday. I banished the memory of smoldering chickens at the Ashby dump, my first attempt at farming.

One day, however, when cows started plopping along Winchendon Road, I suddenly reached the end of my cattle baron aspirations. The animals had nudged open my stylish pole gate, tails waving like pennants, and clip-clopped toward oat fields, lawns and ornamental yards. My young son Samuel, with the hope of heading them off, hopped in our Jeep, but only scared them through more fences.

After about a week, we had roped and dragged home most of our bovines. But three steers still roamed the urban wilds of New Hampshire. One tramped through a neighbor's screened building, costing me $500 in compensation. The steer disappeared for a few days, but we hired a man with a beagle to track the beast to ground. The tracker's second dog, a bulldog, grabbed the steer by the nose and held it still while we tied the animal up.

The other two steers cavorted free of fences for months until a rancher told us they grazed his pasture every evening. My son-in-law, Lloyd, was able to shoot one steer, but the rifle report sent the other one into the woods nearby. We dressed out our downed steer and hauled the meat home. The runaway eventually ended up in another man's freezer.

Only one lawsuit caught up with me. A cranky farmer said that my renegades had trampled his oat field — he settled for $1,500. The next fall I had Lloyd shoot all the remaining cows in our pasture. We gutted, skinned and quartered them and took the meat to the butcher.

I am finally convinced that any Finnish "ranching gene" simply skipped me. Since our happy days on Wind Swept Acres, I have often dined upon chicken and steak, but few of the critters were raised by Marty Seppala.

Ascension at finn hill

❧❧❧

I could never have dreamed so big or challenged life with so much force, except for the backing of the girl who hopped in my '41 Ford and captured my heart.

"Where we goin,' Marty?"

For 35 years, young Barbara Frigard's words defined her role in my life, inspiring me to explore opportunities that I never could have seized without her. Only Barbara knew the panicked Marty, the worried Marty, the frustrated Marty, the romantic Marty. I valued my wife's quiet counsel over all the business consultants I have ever known. Often, Barbara was God's voice to me when I faced difficult decisions in my life.

After three years serving on the Ashby school board, I decided *not* to run for governor of the state of New Hampshire. I was a "shoo in," according to my politically savvy friend and partner, Sam Tamposi. I felt I would be carving up my life into too many pieces: stumping for office, expanding S&A and maintaining a growing family. Barbara let the buck stop with me after consulting with her — and she never berated me over choices I made that affected our future.

When President George H. W. Bush attended our annual Seppala & Aho barbecue, I introduced Barbara with pride, though she was more comfortable away from the spotlight. Even so, she was always on my arm when I needed her at social gatherings.

When I was wrong, Barbara said more without words than if she spoke aloud. We had two driveways at our Wind Swept Acres, and the steepest one we used infrequently. One evening, Barbara and I sat in my new Jeep, ready to visit neighborhood friends, the Olsons, who lived a mile away. This winter evening, I suddenly decided to use the steep *back* driveway for our exit.

I spun out a bit, eased toward the "ski hill" and Barbara's hands suddenly clawed the dashboard.

The best is yet to come

"Marty, it's too icy to go this way!"

As we descended, I patiently explained how adept I was at handling rigs on ice, but shut up halfway down as the tires lost their grip on the ice. Faster and faster we slid. I jammed the brakes and spun the steering wheel, completely out of control. We slued sideways and slammed a row of trees at the bottom of the hill. I shut off the engine, and we sat silent for a few seconds.

"You okay?"

Barbara nodded.

"Let's walk to the Olsons, shall we?"

I talked a little on the way, justifying, then finally confessing, but Barbara never said a single word. The Olsons loved the story and gave us a ride home late that evening.

Our children and I benefited from Barbara's rare gift of nurturing relationships into strong lifetime friendships. An example of this was Ted and Nancy Sarkela.

When the yearly Apostolic Lutheran Convention convened on the West Coast, we stayed with the Sarkelas. When the church convention gathered in the East, the Sarkelas stayed with us.

Barbara and Nancy had much in common: Finnish language, food and culture; strong Apostolic Lutheran ties; similar personalities (forceful, hospitable and fastidious); children about the same age (Ted and Nancy had nine kids); and ambitious, hardheaded Finnish businessmen for husbands.

Ted Sarkela Builders manufactured and installed prefabricated homes, from foundation to rooftop. Their plant was located in Hockinson, Washington, and like the Seppalas, the Sarkela boys and girls had absorbed their parents' work ethic. Their fathers immediately plugged them into positions (menial ones) to learn the business. The Seppala girls in the East and Sarkela girls in the West plotted their rendezvous by telephone, and both of our families couldn't wait to see one another at the yearly church functions.

Ascension at finn hill

And, of course, we dads and moms contemplated our families forever linked by possible marriage unions of our boys and girls someday, if God willed it.

৵৵৵

For us Seppalas, even our vacation bungalow had to be *big*. One inviting feature that drew us to Granite Lake, near Stoddard, New Hampshire, was the clearest water we had ever seen. A two-story cottage, built 50 feet from the lake's edge, had been used as a tourist camp. Spacious upstairs bedrooms, a roomy kitchen and living room with a fireplace clinched the deal for Barbara and me. After purchasing the camp, the first thing I built was a sauna for warming up after a cool swim.

My penchant to improve wherever I lived got me in trouble with a Stoddard selectman when I hauled in loads of sand to create a better beach. I also buried a bunch of rock. But after one visit, he saw how professionally we had enhanced the area and left us alone.

The lake became our vacation home for years and a place for all our families to build wonderful friendships. Barbara and I began to take stock of our future when we relaxed at our Granite Lake getaway. Some of our children had married and moved far away from our Wind Swept notions, with little thought about the dreams of their middle-aged parents. It was time for Barbara and me to begin pondering how our lives were changing. We had four girls and two boys left at home, out of our 17.

Barbara and I envied the shorebirds who pointed formations south, and we decided to follow their example. We made a few trips to Florida to test the waters with Papa and Mumu, and it suited all of us. Papa's lungs seemed stronger immediately, and Mumu loved the warm weather, too.

It seemed wherever I went, excitement followed. Jonathan

landed his general contractor's license in Florida, and this opened up a whole new region for Seppala & Aho.

We established a construction "beachhead" there and targeted wealthy patrons who wanted exclusive condominiums with ocean views. Dune Deck and Emerade were just two of the midrise condos we built on the ocean.

In 1978, Barbara and I made our move to Florida for good. In cold New Hampshire, Barbara's health had turned sketchy in winter, like she carried an unseen burden at the end of each day. In Florida, this health burden seemed lighter.

Daniel ran the business in New Hampshire after I left. Wanda lived in Florida already, and Samuel moved his family to Florida. Nate and his wife and kids followed soon after. We continued to build condos on the coast, and they sold well. We built 25 condominiums in Lantana with a pool house, sauna and pool and finished them by 1980. These were called the Town Pines, and several friends and relatives purchased condos there.

When we told our family and friends that Barbara and I would be flying to Israel, a lifelong dream, everyone rejoiced with us. I tied up loose ends at S&A. Barbara shepherded our travel preparations. She also kept an appointment for a full physical examination.

Barbara's zest and energetic footsteps wearied long before sunset these days. She had discovered a lump under her arm, and symptoms conveyed a strong possibility that she suffered from a form of cancer.

"Should we cancel our trip to Israel?" I asked the physician.

"No, Marty. By all means, make your trip. We'll do a biopsy when you return." His tone seemed resigned, almost ominous, whether he meant it to be or not. From that moment, I braced for a struggle that none of my business savvy or life experience had prepared me for.

On our last pilgrimage together, I reached deeply into

God's grace for daily strength and empathy to serve my beautiful Barbara. In Jerusalem, we walked the same streets that Jesus walked and stopped for shade beneath trees at the Mount of Olives. We traveled to the Garden of Gethsemane and stood on the sands beside the Sea of Galilee. With 23 others in our group, we shared a spiritual journey I shall always remember. Every moment in the Holy Land felt intimate and meaningful.

Jesus' Garden Tomb held a significance that neither of us spoke about. Before we left the Promised Land, Barbara passed through one of Jerusalem's gates, and I wrote a caption for one of my last photographs of her: "Through the gate, into the city."

We never discussed her departure from this world while in the weeks we toured the Promised Land, but deep down I knew.

かかか

I left Israel with a feeling of angst after speaking with a scholarly man who rejected Christ and the religion of his forefathers. "Let me tell you what we Jews believe," he said. "You say God created man? We say man created God."

A fear that God is only a fictitious, cosmic character seeps into the consciousness of intellectual young people today, even in our churches. Those of us who have served Jesus over the generations must tell our stories of God's interactions with us, tying in steel to strengthen their spiritual foundations.

Experience affirms faith.

At JFK Medical Center the doctor opened the door to the waiting room. He fiddled with a stethoscope on his chest, his face clouded. His news wasn't what I wanted to hear.

"The cancer is inoperable, Marty. It has spread to her vital organs."

My knees felt weak, and I needed to sit. "No hope, then?" I asked, my voice cracking.

"One in five cases of cancer actually cures itself, without

any treatment at all but …" The doctor shook his head.

Barbara and I agreed that we should gather the children and tell them. I caught up with as many as I could reach and invited them to the house. It seemed strange that we weren't discussing a business investment, or a vacation, or an upcoming marriage.

Tears flowed after we told them about her cancer diagnosis. But Barbara, in her typically down-to-earth fashion, said, "Don't you all bury me *before* I die!"

Seeing Mother so peaceful within her crisis made it easier for all of us to accept God's will. Barbara did little to change her lifestyle until the effects of chemotherapy forced her to make major adjustments in her schedule.

After the sale of our home, we started a new development called Finn Hill, in Lantana. On 14 lots, several relatives built their homes. Mike and my sister Elaine built right next door to us, and Samuel and Ruthie, his wife, built across the street. Later, Josh, Alice, Daniel, Judy, Rod and Debi built homes with their families there, too.

I rushed to build our home so that Barbara could enjoy it. We designed it with four bedrooms, four baths, a large kitchen and den overlooking a covered porch that led to a pool and orchard with fruit trees. A sunken living room and dining room accommodated Barbara's never-ending queue of concerned guests. Children in bathing suits and gym shorts careened between the pool and a basketball court I built to keep them occupied.

I cut back all my administrative duties at S&A and treasured the moments when Barbara had strength enough to perch at our big Rogers Organ, playing and singing hymns with family and friends. While she talked with visitors, no hint of dread slipped into Barbara's conversations about leaving earth. Losing her hair, bouts of uncontrollable coughing, struggling to breathe, pain in her joints — Barbara believed that her suffering preceded her triumphant entry into heaven. She had nurtured many in her life, and now I watched Jesus nourish her spirit, preparing her for a new plane of existence.

I had carried Barbara to her bed one day and noticed that she was deep in thought. "You've been quiet today, darling. What have you been thinking about?"

She answered me a little distractedly, but with a smile. "About death, Marty."

My chest felt leaden, and I couldn't speak for a few seconds. "Do you think death is close? Do you want me to call the children so that you can talk to them?"

She took a deep breath and nodded. "Yes. It's very close."

By phone, I caught up with the kids, one after the other. From Barbara's bed, she gave our son or daughter the same preparatory message to comfort them: "God's peace. I'm going home now. God's peace."

Before I hung up the phone, I told them, "You fly here as fast as you can! Mom's going to be leaving shortly," then called the next one.

Barbara began to dance.

Her arms reached upward, and her legs moved rhythmically to music I could not detect.

"Multitudes! Look at that! They're so happy, and they have their hands raised!" Barbara's voice spoke clearly and strong. "Come! Come! Everybody!"

I stood upon holy ground. Jesus allowed me to experience the joyful vision of Barbara's welcome. I understood her imploring: "Come. Everybody!" Her call reached past the walls of our home and into the streets, an invitation from a soon-departing soul.

"God showed me heaven, Marty."

Barbara suddenly seemed weak again, and I adjusted the oxygen tubes for her to breathe easier. "He'll be showing me more before he calls me home," she said.

The best is yet to come

I lost my Barbara that day. She still *lived*, but her desire to see Jesus surpassed all need for earthly companionship from a husband.

Every morning after this first vision, I awoke to, "Maybe Jesus will come for me today!"

God reserved six days for us to celebrate sending Barbara home. A continual stream of people came to see her, and when our pastor Tretten dropped by, she shocked him with: "Could you please go tell Jesus to just come and get me …"

She took a turn for the worse one morning, and I rushed her to the hospital. The next day she felt better, but seemed sad and serious.

"I've seen hell, Marty. It really *is* a place of eternal aloneness. No one should ever have to go there. Such darkness and solitude," she said. I'll never forget the pain in her eyes and voice.

All my children except one (Debi hated to stay on the West Coast, but was hours away from giving birth) were able to experience Mother's rejoicing, so close to leaving for heaven. A couple dozen of our sons, daughters, wives, husbands and children slept all over our house on Finn Hill, waiting expectantly.

On the sixth day after her vision of heaven, I left briefly to buy groceries for our hungry family of Finns. On the drive home from the supermarket, I felt a sense of great anticipation, and I knew the day was at hand.

When I returned, Wanda sang a song, originating from the Holy Spirit, especially for her mother. An air of excitement pulsed through the house, along with our normal hubbub of lunch, dishes and children.

Suddenly, my daughter-in-law, Rita, so attentive to Mother, called to me. Barbara was speaking aloud, and everyone gathered close.

"I hear his footsteps. He's coming now," Mother said.

Ascension at finn hill

No one broke into tears. Happy, heavenly calm settled on us all.

During most of these last days Barbara suffered little pain, but when I asked if she had discomfort she said quietly, "Yes."

"Where, darling?"

"*All* over ..."

As I watched her face, her eyelids never closed, but I knew she was "absent from the body, present with the Lord." She left her suffering behind.

Mike Demoulas came to the house right away to pay respects, and our New Ipswich church could not contain the crowd who gathered to celebrate her passing. She was buried at Ashby Cemetery.

My months of grieving finally ended, when the wife of my youth fled to the arms of her Savior.

ॐ ॐ ॐ

At 57 years old, hard-driving Martin Seppala gazed upon an uncharted horizon, confident in God, but somehow drained of vitality. For the first time, I understood how my mother felt when she lost my father. At night, a waterfall of memories poured through me. I lay awake, trying to wrap my mind around the truth: I would never again see Barbara humming hymns as she baked bread. No one would be waiting up after midnight to rejoice with me as I crowed over conquering a construction job.

My earthly destiny had changed. I felt more "grandpa" than businessman now. My fulfillment lay in God, enhanced by a strong ambition to mentor my progeny. God had certified this high and noble vocation, and it was my "portion" until I joined Barbara.

But, why did I feel like I had booked a long, uncomfortable flight with a cut-rate airline?

The best is yet to come

My daughter Annie comforted me with meals at her gracious home for some time after the funeral, but anyone who knew me took note of the dark circles under my eyes each morning. My one solace: seeing 14 of my children and my bevy of grandkids together at our old New Ipswich church on Sunday.

At the services, a beautiful sense of holiday anticipation percolated throughout, and when the services ended, my old friends hugged my neck and stood around, attempting to console me. But they weren't the ones I needed. I yearned to be close to my sons, daughters and grandchildren, so I sidled away as quickly as I could. On the covered porch, my chest tightened as I surveyed the parking lot, nearly empty.

Everyone in my family had simply *gone*. My hands deep in coat pockets, I walked to my car. Behind the cold steering wheel, I can't recall ever feeling so lonely on a gray winter day.

Not a single invitation for lunch.

I decided to take my sorry soul to a nostalgic place where no one could hear me cry: our Granite Lake cottage.

On the road toward Stoddard, I had a good talk with Jesus, who quietly listened to my woes. At Granite Lake, I let myself inside the cottage and into Barbara's presence. She was everywhere — the kitchen, the bedrooms, the den. I warmed the cottage with a roaring fire and sat down to stare at the flames, tears streaming.

Marty, when I'm gone, I want you to find a strong Christian woman, and marry her.

Often, during our 35 years, my habit of tuning out Barbara's explicit instructions landed me in hot water, so when her words came back to me this time, I listened.

"Lord, is this your will?"

I wasn't happy *alone.* Nor would I ever be. That evening at Granite Lake, my trajectory changed, like on the harrowing commuter flight I had never forgotten.

Ascension at finn hill

We had taken off from a family-owned landing strip in Jaffrey, where we kept S&A's Cessna inline twin-engine plane. It seated up to four passengers, plus a pilot, and on our return trip from New York City, we ran close to an unexpected thunderstorm. We rerouted our flight path 180 degrees to the closest available airport. As we descended toward a Rhode Island runway, the squall tracked closer to the plane, and a buzzer screamed that the landing gear had jammed. Our pilot issued a distress call when the squall caught us and the radio went dead.

"We can make it one more time around the field, but then I *have* to land," our pilot warned, tapping the fuel gauge.

We never heard the landing gear drop into position, and all of us tensed and strained to keep the nose *up* (as if we could). We descended until we heard the screech of rubber on wet pavement, relieved and thanking God.

After Barbara's passing, I circled in a threatening storm of loneliness, but at Granite Lake God showed me a field of dreams where I could safely land.

Find a strong Christian woman, and marry her.

But who on this earth could put up with me? She would have to love Jesus dearly and have an Apostolic Lutheran background. Have a sense of adventure and ambition. Understand business. Love my children and grandchildren. *And* enjoy my peculiar sense of humor.

The face of only one woman drifted across my mind, and I knew Barbara would heartily approve.

Nancy.

Starting a partnership, Hjalmer Aho and Martin Seppala

Family picture (1971) Back row: Samuel, Annie, Jonathan, Daniel, Joel, Wanda; Middle row: Nathan, Sandy, Barbara holding Marci, Martin holding Millie, Debbie;
Front row: Benjamin, Joshua, Mindy, Heidi, Matthew, Amos

Seppala & Aho Construction Company, Inc.
President, Martin Seppala

Seppala & Aho Construction Company, Inc.
New Ipswich, New Hampshire

Seppala & Aho office back view

To Marty Seppala
with best wishes

Portsmouth, NH Barbecue with Vice
President George Bush, Bill Kivela,
Daniel Seppala and Marty Seppala

Barbara and Marty Seppala

Wind Swept Acres

Friends visiting at Wind Swept Acres.
Janie Sarkela, Mindy Seppala, Marci Seppala,
Millie Seppala, Nonna Sarkela, Alice Sarkela

Chapter seven
Vows and vision

In the mid-1800s, children in Hockinson, Washington, spoke the languages of the Norsemen who had sailed from islands near Sweden to settle in the Pacific Coast forestlands. For six generations, a Finnish pride of identity has defined the Hockinson community, where Ted and Nancy Sarkela pioneered a thriving construction company.

Ted married Nancy Christopher, an ambitious Minnesota girl shaped by her family's climb out of depression-era hardships. Their Apostolic Lutheran heritage set Ted and Nancy's spiritual roots deep. Their love for God, their children and for one another steered a course for a bright future together.

Ted and Nancy added one more child to their eight when Ted's mother died. Ted's mother had left Ted's brother, 22-month-old Bruce, to be raised and loved as one of Nancy's own. Bruce, Naomi, Rodney, David, Steven, John, Alice, Janie and Norma grew up in the tight-knit Christian Finnish community.

But when Ted's brother, Don, passed away from primary biliary cirrhosis, a progressive liver disease, Nancy's role in life began to change. Though Ted appeared robust and strong, doctors warned that he showed signs of the same progressive illness that struck his brother. Miraculously, Ted barely slowed his pace during the two years before his one good kidney began to fail.

Ted and Nancy's faith in God remained strong throughout the months of medical treatments, and when Ted heard of Barbara Seppala's terminal cancer, he pondered their shared destinies.

The best is yet to come

"Looks like Barbara and I'll be seeing each other in heaven pretty soon," he told Nancy matter-of-factly one day. Toward the end of Ted's illness, going home to be with his Savior seldom left his mind.

On March 27, 1982, Ted answered God's immediate call to rule and reign with Jesus. He left Nancy and his children to follow his brother into eternity a year before the Seppalas celebrated Barbara's bittersweet departure.

The heavy responsibilities of raising two elementary school girls and a teenage daughter *and* gathering in the reins of Sarkela Builders (later known as American Home Builders) fell to Nancy. Not only did she face life without the husband of her youth, but national turmoil tossed Sarkela Builders into white caps of uncertainty. Like torrents grinding through the Columbia River Gorge, high interest rates eroded the expansion of businesses all over the West Coast.

During the recession of 1982, the Sarkela corporation included warehouses, a manufacturing plant for prefabricated homes, a lumber yard, paint shop and several pieces of heavy equipment for onsite deliveries and construction. Their payroll included 25 supervisory staff and laborers.

With God's help, Nancy and her supervisors trimmed down overhead and sold off assets, streamlining the business to survive the recession. Prime interest rates hovered near 20 percent. Dozens of savings and loan companies closed their doors. The demand for new homes dwindled to a trickle. President Jimmy Carter lost his presidency, and President Ronald Reagan assumed leadership of a nation in financial and international chaos.

During the month that Ted traded in his active but frail "vessel" for a heavenly one, two of his sons married beautiful soul mates here on earth. Of much greater impact than corporate expansion, the Sarkela family continued to grow healthy and effective in Christ.

Vows and vision

Mornings were hectic for Nancy as she juggled her new life to accommodate school commutes, church services, homemaking and her duties as a CEO. Weekends seemed empty and lonely without the familiar, caring voice of a husband to discuss choices.

A year after Ted's passing, the corporate world had buried Nancy in a morass of decisions. She waited for God's direction concerning her personal future as well. Naomi, her oldest daughter, lived in the area with her husband and children. But Nancy's sons had moved away to start their own families. In a few years, the three girls at home would find good men as well, God willing.

Nancy Sarkela looked forward to mentoring grandchildren in a fulfilling, sweet life, even if she ended up living it all alone.

ॐॐॐ

The Father planned it all.

It seemed way too soon at first, but after God showed me whom I should seek as a life companion, a strange sense of destiny drove me forward. I left the New Hampshire cottage with a mandate, as clear as the pristine waters of our beautiful Granite Lake. A blueprint for winning Nancy Sarkela slowly began to unfold.

Considering our situations, Nancy and I had lost touch somewhat, though our girls were phone pals, airing Sarkela and Seppala broadcasts periodically. And through the Finnish grapevine, I was able to shrink the distance between east and west by inquiring of folks who knew both of our families.

"Oh, yes. It's wonderful — Nancy is dating. A Finnish gentleman from the West Coast is courting her," a well-meaning woman informed me.

My heart sank like an iron bolt tossed in a lake. I had to act fast or Nancy might fall for someone else!

The best is yet to come

I confided in my children. "If I don't marry Nancy, I'm not going to get married at all. It's Nancy or nobody."

At 58 years old, I had only one speed: *full throttle*. Even now (at 85), I have one approach to ventures: I'm *all* in or *all* out. Thank God, Nancy Sarkela overlooked my impassioned, impatient attempts to win her and recognized God's hand in our future together. It happened that the Apostolic Lutheran Church convention was held in Fitchburg, Massachusetts, in 1983, and through the grapevine, I picked a juicy bunch of news: Nancy would be flying in to attend the conference.

Nancy knew me as Barbara's "livewire" husband and as a family friend. She had seldom seen the earnest, thoughtful side of Marty Seppala. Only God could transform our friendship into something more. What would Nancy think if I told her about my Granite Lake "revelation"?

Providence moved quickly. One morning I "happened" to drive past the cemetery at Ashby, where Barbara was laid to rest. The Apostolic Lutheran Church meetings were about to begin, and as a Finnish interpreter and lay speaker, I would be attending commencement forums that lasted all day.

At Barbara's gravesite, I noticed Elmi, Barbara's sister, standing with none other than Nancy Sarkela, paying respects. I sat for a moment, awash in misgivings. The woman I believed God had shown me to be my lifetime partner stood at my wife's graveside. When the two women noticed me sitting some distance away, they came over.

After greetings and a little small talk, Elmi said, "Nancy needs a car today to get around town. Can you spare yours?"

I noticed Nancy frown, like Elmi had given her a taste of something that she couldn't quite identify.

"Oh, no …"

My chivalry took over. "I insist! It's the least I can do, Nancy. Just drop me off at the preachers' meetings, and the car's all yours." She gave in, reluctantly.

Vows and vision

I drove my Lincoln Continental, Nancy in the front seat next to me, at quarter speed to the Fitchburg meeting, much like my uncle Bill had driven his Model A. I was fumbling for small talk most of the way. Then I suddenly took a deep breath.

"I hear you're dating someone back home."

Her long silence *pinched* me for being so awkward, but she replied graciously.

"Yes, I am."

I was treading on very thin ice now, but I couldn't stop myself. At conventions, Finns congregate like bees, and Nancy was especially popular. This might be my last chance to speak my heart to her alone.

Do it now!

"How serious are you about him? I mean, *are* you serious? Before you answer me, Nancy, I'll let you know that I am very interested in you."

Interested? Was that the right word? Oh, God!

Nancy answered me tactfully, like a lawyer on the opposing end of a contract. Her words nearly broke my heart. "Marty, we've known each other a long time. Can't we just be friends?"

I've been interpreting Finnish sermons for English-speaking congregations for 30 years, and I knew exactly what "Can't we just be friends?" meant: "You're too late, buddy."

I opened the door to my Lincoln and distractedly instructed her on how to drive, like she was a 15 year old. She seemed overly polite as she drove off, and I stood with a big Bible under my arm like a jilted schoolboy, staring after her.

"Lord, thy will …" I said in my troubled spirit, wondering about my Granite Lake "revelation." Our ALC convention lasted for days, so I hoped for another time to share my heart with Nancy. I would need to be quite convincing, since *my whole earthly future and hers* was at stake.

Somehow, I took up a place near Nancy at every informal gathering during convention. Little by little, she overlooked my

The best is yet to come

awkward overtures, and we settled into a comfortable friendship again. Our Christian friends watched and encouraged us.

One evening, Nancy asked me for counsel, and I felt honored that she brought me into her confidence.

"Someone has offered to buy the Sarkela Builders plant, but he wants to "part-trade" for land near the Columbia River. What do you think?"

We talked for some time about her situation, and I could feel the connection between us growing stronger. Her style of management and mine differed somewhat. Hers was thoughtful and analytical; mine, progressive and bold. Between convention meetings, my daughter Heidi and her husband, Steve, invited us to The Old Mill Restaurant. Norma, Nancy's 10-year-old daughter, came, too.

"Norma, can I be your daddy just for today?" I asked as she sat on my lap. She smiled and nodded. I prayed that God would grant Nancy the insight to recognize my strong commitment and the love that was stirring for her children, as well as for her.

One evening at Bill and Cora Peterson's home, we sang and recorded our American-style hymns of rejoicing for Ivar Lampa, a Finnish pastor who visited from Sweden. Years before, Ted Sarkela had phoned to recommend Pastor Lampa as a special speaker, and I had invited Ivar to stay with us as he toured our churches for preaching engagements. We became great friends.

Nancy was staying with Hjalmer Aho's family, and when it was time to leave Bill and Cora's house, I offered to take Nancy and little Norma back to the Ahos' place. As I parked, Norma hopped out of the car and bounded up the steps, leaving Nancy and I alone for a moment. I took one last shot at declaring my intentions.

I locked the car doors. "Nancy, I can't let you go. I'm going to keep you ..."

Vows and vision

How else could I show her that she captivated *me*?

"Mama, are you coming?" Norma had reappeared at Nancy's window. I unlocked the doors.

I yearned to know if Nancy shared my feelings, but I drove away wondering if this might be the final scene in an unsatisfying drama. Little time remained to reinforce that I was serious about courting her. A day or two later, after saying our goodbyes, Nancy flew off to Washington, leaving me to worry over what she was thinking. I set my sights on pursuing Nancy in August at the next ALC meetings, scheduled at Hockinson.

That summer, I tried to adjust to living alone and raising my son Josh and three daughters Mindy, Marci and Millie. I targeted new challenges in S&A, but my unclaimed heart drifted somewhere between the East and West Coasts. At every opportunity, I tuned in to the grapevine for Nancy news. My daughter Debbie and her family lived in Hockinson, and my children conversed from our home phone with Nancy's daughters. I was well positioned to discover up-to-the-minute reports concerning Nancy and her "West Coast guy."

One evening, earth-shaking intelligence streaked across 3,000 miles and hit the headlines at Finn Hill: Nancy Sarkela had rejected advances from my competition! I immediately fired off a card expressing my hopes for a relationship, and Nancy showed the card to her sister-in-law, Gloria, who knew me pretty well.

Gloria just shook her head. "This isn't the last you'll hear from Marty. He's coming your way, like a Mack truck ..."

ॐॐॐ

Road trip!
In August, for the fall Apostolic Lutheran convention, Marci, Josh, Millie and I loaded up luggage and sped toward the West Coast. Our only delay was to stop and pick up Mindy on

the way at Bruce Crossing, Michigan, where she had been visiting friends.

In Hockinson, we unpacked our gear at my daughter Debbie's and son-in-law Lloyd's beautiful home. I tried to politely settle down, but everyone knew that I had only one person on my mind.

"Nancy! How are you? Do you have the sauna on?"

I hoped that my first foray by telephone might clue me in about her feelings: A Finn welcomed a guest with a hot sauna. A *cold* one was a courteous way to say, "I'd rather not have company, right now."

On the other end of the line, Nancy held me in suspense for what seemed like an eternity, then said, "No, the sauna's not fired up right now, Marty."

My 3,000-mile bubble almost burst, until she continued, "… but I'll turn it on."

A sweeter, more fulfilling welcome I've seldom experienced. Nancy had much at stake. Major business decisions. Three children to raise who needed a loving father. A need for a fulfilling relationship with someone who treated her family with respect and love. And the desire for a soul mate to enhance her God-given gifts in the years to come.

I had filled the miles during our cross-country trip to Washington with discussions with Nancy (all in my head). Now, I could finally introduce her to the real me: not the businessman or gregarious Finn she and Ted had known, but the man I was inside — flawed but hopeful. Impatient, but willing to change my ways. Knowing my God-inspired purpose and, like her, needing a helpmate who complemented my ministry.

During my sojourn in Hockinson for the ALC meetings, I spent time with Nancy to reveal my hopes for the two of us. At her home, God began kindling a romance between us as we shared our heartaches and our dreams for the future.

Vows and vision

On a trip to the Columbia River, we hiked to the top of Multnomah Falls, and during the long trip back down, we paused to rest on a bench. Hikers of many nationalities came and went, and a woman paused to talk to us. I launched briefly into our history, and she seemed enthralled.

"We've been friends for a long time! Recently, we lost our spouses within a year of each other. I plan to ask Nancy to be my wife. Don't you think we'd make a great couple?"

Nancy didn't register the least bit of embarrassment. I was thrilled to feel that my "chosen one" warmed to the adventure ahead. I had been grieving Barbara's two-year illness and final passing. Nancy had grieved during Ted's illness and for a year after. It was time for both of us to release the past and lay hold of God's exciting tomorrows.

"Go for it, Nancy!" the woman exclaimed and, laughing, strode down the trail.

I took Nancy's hand. "If you marry me I'll try to make you the happiest wife in the world. See! Even a complete stranger can see we were meant for each other!"

Nancy and I attended services back in Hockinson, and I watched her between services as she organized the meals for hundreds of guests. One evening, as Nancy stood over a massive pot of potatoes, I whispered in her ear, "When you marry me, you won't have to work so hard." But arduous work didn't scare her, nor did she ever hold me to that *hopeful, yet rash* promise.

I left Nancy in Washington State and traveled home to Florida with my children, feeling like a teenager, fighting the urge to call her at every fuel stop. And back at Finn Hill, I couldn't blame Marci, my daughter, and Janie, Nancy's daughter, for running up the phone bills anymore. Their smitten parents were suddenly the worst offenders.

Over the months I arranged my schedule to make several trips to the West Coast. Every moment together confirmed my

The best is yet to come

God-given insight at Granite Lake: I would be the happiest man in the world if this woman consented to be Nancy *Seppala*.

On one of my trips to Hockinson, Janie overheard us talking about Nancy and her girls coming to check out the "lay of the land" at Finn Hill. Before Nancy or I could get to a phone, Janie had airline reservations nailed down, and by October, the four "inspectors" were on their way to Florida. For months, Marci and Janie had schemed about uniting our two families. Now their prayers were close to sealing the deal.

I was nervous as a cat when I met the chief investigator and her protégés at the airport. What if the girls didn't like our Finn Hill house or our town of Lantana? What if Nancy didn't like the diamond I had picked out?

"I see coal spots. Do you have any others?" I grumbled, and the jeweler had rolled his eyes. I didn't blame him. I couldn't seem to find the quality ring I wanted, a ring that would show Nancy how much I valued her.

Finally, in Fitchburg, I found the perfect solitaire diamond ring. As for day-to-day work at S&A, I couldn't seem to focus much.

Finally they arrived. I drove Nancy, Janie, Alice and Norma to the home of my son-in-law Sam and daughter Ruthie, who lived right across the street from me on Finn Hill. The Sarkela ladies were warmly welcomed.

It was October 8th, Nancy's birthday, when I took her to dinner at The Breakers Hotel, a five-star dining experience. Then we strolled the boardwalk on Singer Island, and during a romantic pause beneath a thatched hut, I handed her the gift box with the promise of my heart inside.

Nancy's eyes shone bright, but she seemed to be waiting for something else to happen.

"Aren't you going to ask me if I'll *wear* this?"

Oops.

I had asked her to marry me so many times over the

Vows and vision

previous months that I actually figured she knew the question already! I rescued the moment, like snatching a hammer before it plummeted eight stories.

"Will you wear my ring? Will you marry me, Nancy?"

She set my heart at ease. I smiled inside, knowing that this woman would never be *predictable.*

Melding two complex businesses, two large homes, six girls and a son would take every ounce of our Sarkela and Seppala management skills combined. After our official engagement, we began liquidating some of Nancy's holdings and expanding others. We reorganized her West Coast business and renamed it American Home Builders, preparing for the anticipated upswing in the economy. Small businesses all over the country seemed to be looking for better times ahead.

ॐॐॐ

Two months after Finn Hill passed the Sarkela women's official inspection, my children and I were back in Hockinson for a December wedding. Ivar Lampa, the Swedish friend of the Sarkelas and Seppalas, preached a short sermon before our vows. Nancy's elder pastor at Hockinson Apostolic Lutheran Church, Reverend Forshaug, performed our marriage ceremony, and I felt honored to have my son Daniel as best man and Nancy's oldest daughter, Naomi, as matron of honor.

Absorbed in Nancy's beauty, I barely recall the sermon and little of the vows. Nancy's flowing lace cream-colored wedding gown, the delicate off-white decor of the Hockinson church and the fragrant pink roses everywhere captured me in a mythical vision. Even my brown suit fit the setting (a suit that Nancy had carefully chosen). Our six girls, Nancy's Janie, Alice and Norma, with my own Marcie, Millie and Mindy, sang a song that summed up our romance and commitment from the beginning: "The Father Planned It All."

The best is yet to come

I was a well-known and (generally) loved ringleader for shenanigans, and my new wife could not escape reaping what I had sowed at many a gathering. After cutting the cake and socializing a bit, we headed off to change clothes at Naomi's house. This gave a dozen or more giggling, guffawing relatives and friends time to gather forces.

"We'll buy 'em off at the A&W Root Beer Stand," I told Nancy, who snuggled close as I unsuccessfully tried to lose our entourage. Boisterous, honking wedding guests trailed in our wake, and after bribing everyone with root beer floats, we waited for the troublemakers to lose interest. It didn't happen. None of them actually followed us upstairs *into* our hotel room, but they feasted upon our dismay for as long as possible!

The memories of our special day, with so many wonderful friends and family, remain vivid and satisfying after 28 years. We often attend weddings of children, grandchildren and friends and easily slip into our own recollections during their ceremonies. A squeezed hand from me and Nancy's answering smile reminds us of our first pages in a chapter of new beginnings.

From Washington State, we drove to San Francisco to spend a little time sightseeing. Next we flew to Honolulu where an ocean-side hotel room waited for us. We toured Oahu, then flew to Maui. The scenery, the food, the flora and fauna were breathtaking, but not as grand and surprising as what we discovered at home.

Grand: Rod and Debi Sarkela had our grandson Shawn waiting for us!

Surprising: Nancy had left our seven kids her American Express card to buy a few Christmas gifts. They racked up a bill for $10,000!

Moving Nancy and her "treasures" across 48 states to settle at Finn Hill took very careful planning: boxing up belongings, flying children cross country and hauling the remainder of

Vows and vision

furnishings. Good friends, like Bill and Carol Inman, helped us move.

We worked hard to ease our three girls into their new environment: school, church and friendships. We remodeled our garage into bedrooms and a bathroom (the most popular room in any house with children). We now had a total of six bedrooms.

More grandchildren came. Zackie, Sam and Ruthie's son, lived right across the street. He played at our house nearly as much as his own. We had nearly sold all of the homes and lots on Finn Hill when Nancy and I decided to build the last spec home at the end of one of the streets. We happily jumped into the project during the first months of our marriage.

Nancy redesigned blueprints with a personal flair, and I admired her handiwork. I ramrodded the grading work, leveling the pad for a foundation. But when I called for trucks to haul in material to level out the back of the lot, I unknowingly set in motion a chain of consequences every builder dreads.

One morning, without my approval, my backhoe operator decided to dig a large hole a few feet away from nearby railroad tracks in order to bury leftover debris. Without calling for a locate (testing above ground for buried cables), he had no idea what mysteries lay beneath his iron claw. Where he dug, MCI Communications had installed fiber optic cables and phone lines connecting the entire South Florida region to the rest of the world.

Nancy and I were returning home in the evening when we noticed a commotion behind the spec house site. Red, blue and yellow flashing lights reflected off the windows of half a dozen parked police and Florida State vehicles. Communications personnel in coveralls and hard hats scurried across the lot, like termites on a woodpile.

My heart nearly stopped beating when I noticed my

backhoe parked nearby. My first instinct was to beat a retreat, like I had from the town hall after the smoldering chickens at the Ashby dump incident. But I stayed and faced the music.

My backhoe operator had severed the MCI trunk line, as well as shredded a mass of arteries that pumped millions of bits and bytes of information. Some of these cables had connected national defense installations, and the cost of repair would reach millions of dollars per day.

Day and night, workmen and technicians reconnected lines. Police guarded the area, and our insurance premiums rose accordingly. I never asked the total cost of repairs.

We sold the completed spec house to an employee and barely broke even.

≈≈≈

In our first eventful year together, Nancy and I charted a course toward semi-retirement. We hoped to ease into our new lifestyle, closing up shop during the hot summers at Finn Hill and moving north to New Hampshire. Our family would return to Florida in the fall, in time for school. As our seven children grew up and moved away, we could decide exactly where to concentrate our efforts for ministry.

Money would never be a problem, since our interests were carefully invested and monitored by our sons and daughters. In time, we planned to liquidate many of our holdings and accrue funds to live on, as well as supplement the ministries that God brought to our attention.

Rod had taken over American Home Builders in the West, and at the time, the economy was showing signs of sustained recovery. But another unexpected downturn in the economy occurred, and we decided it was time to liquidate the company. Under Rod's leadership, the plant had grown by leaps and bounds, but the housing market could not keep up with our growth. The banks were helpful in allowing us to settle all debts in a timely, organized manner. Rod and Debi moved to Florida.

Right around our first wedding anniversary, Nancy's yearly physical examination sent a shudder through our entire family. My concern for her health deepened when microscopic traces of blood in urine samples pointed to some problem, and her general practitioner suggested that she get further tests at a hospital.

At her appointment, nurses drew Nancy's blood, and a doctor performed a biopsy while I sat in the waiting room, trying not to relive the day I found out about Barbara's cancer. I had way too much time to think.

When the results came back, the news stunned us both. According to the physician, one of Nancy's kidneys was laced with cancer. I asked for an immediate conference to ask questions.

"Can the cancer be removed by surgery?"

"Mr. Seppala, this cancer is at stage four, so the whole kidney must be extracted. And there is always a possibility that cancer cells may still grow in the area. It's imperative that we get *all* of it."

Nancy and I stared into one another's souls for a few seconds. Then I said wearily, "We should probably get a second opinion before making a decision."

"Well, you've already received your *second* opinion. My associate has examined the same tests, and it's our recommendation that the cancerous kidney be removed." He shuffled papers, waiting for an answer.

"Give us a moment, please, doctor."

We walked into the waiting room, and I couldn't disguise how shaken I was. She, too, had watched a loved one die, and this whole episode seemed like a nightmare neither of us could awaken from. "Honey, if it's stage four, you better have it out," I said, and she took a deep breath, nodding.

The best is yet to come

I found the doctor in his office. "How soon can you operate? I don't want this to spread." We began preparations that same day to have Nancy's cancer-ridden kidney removed. I had been praying from the beginning of her tests, but suddenly I could barely articulate my heartrending petition for God to heal Nancy. The thought of losing her haunted my mind, although, deep in my soul, I knew that God had the situation under control.

The surgeon at Physicians Hospital took out Nancy's kidney, and for weeks afterward, we waited on pins and needles for test results we received periodically. One day, a knock at the door injected our suspense with fresh confusion.

We invited two Florida State investigators inside our home. They sat in our living room and seemed uncomfortable in our best chairs.

"We would like permission to obtain your medical records, Mrs. Seppala. We're opening an investigation into, well, inconsistencies concerning your surgery."

Nancy and I sat beside one another on the sofa, dumbstruck. We stared at the young man and woman. Suddenly, I didn't feel so cordial anymore. I grabbed Nancy's hand to reassure her.

"*What* are you talking about?"

"We believe that something went wrong during the surgery, and you need to contact an attorney to get more information about allegations. We need you to sign these forms stating that you authorize the State of Florida to open a full investigation. Can you do that for us?"

We asked a few more questions that they would not answer, but we signed the documents, anyway. When the State investigators drove away, Nancy and I prayed over the strange cascading events.

A few days after the visit, Nancy's urine samples *still* showed microscopic amounts of blood! We couldn't fathom

Vows and vision

why, and no one at Physicians Hospital satisfactorily answered our concerns. My own blood began to boil as I watched Nancy ride a rollercoaster of emotions.

"Marty, have they taken out the wrong kidney?"

I had no answer. Nancy had exactly the same symptoms that led to her cancer diagnosis in the first place! I was at the end of my patience and decided to get to the bottom of the whole confounding business.

The original operating physician managed to avoid any conferences with us. Now Nancy's distress seemed to be causing dizzy spells. So I took her to another doctor close to home, and he perused her medical records briefly.

"According to your chart, you have a rapidly spreading cancer. It may have been carried by your bloodstream into other parts of your body, including your brain, Mrs. Seppala." He looked kindly at Nancy and at me. I prayed fervently that his unwelcome "potential" diagnosis was some kind of mistake.

"I'll prescribe a couple medications, but if the vertigo persists, in two weeks let's set you up for a brain scan, shall we?"

If I could have taken the worry, the vertigo and the "cancer" upon myself in order to relieve my darling, I would gladly have absorbed every bit.

I lived the next few weeks in a daze, seldom focusing enough to complete important tasks. Though Nancy's vertigo subsided, we were still left with the burden of wondering: Was Nancy's remaining kidney riddled with cancer, too, or had the surgeon taken out the wrong one?

I believe that God directed us to the top urologist at Massachusetts General Hospital. We were told to bring slides of the diseased kidney with us. At Physicians Hospital, the pathology department personnel seemed nervous when we asked for it.

"I'm afraid we cannot find your biopsy slides, Mrs. Seppala."

The best is yet to come

"You better look again. We're not leaving until we have my wife's records," I said, and we sat down to wait. Sometime later, an assistant to the pathologist approached Nancy and me. In her hand was a packet.

"I want you to have this, Mrs. Seppala," she said quietly. Her hands were shaking as she handed Nancy the envelope. "This is the tissue sample from your extracted kidney."

We took the biopsy results to our new doctor at Boston's Mass General, who seemed knowledgeable, both in medical and legal issues. After examining Nancy's tissue slides and making several phone calls, he asked us in for a conference.

"You are the victims of severe malpractice, my friends. The State of Florida will be prosecuting the case. The tissue sample from your removed kidney which I examined shows no sign of cancer. The kidney in your body is fine, too. But your bladder is giving off microscopic benign blood cells. *That* is treatable by medication."

He could see the relief on our faces, but our frowns suggested more questions.

"From what I know, the pathologist at Physicians Hospital misdiagnosed your kidney as cancerous. Then he may have conspired with the surgeon to cover up his mistake. Your kidney that the surgeon removed was *healthy*, I'm afraid. The assistant to the pathologist kept tissue slides of your extracted kidney hidden as evidence so that the State could prosecute the pathologist and hospital. Without this nurse, no one would have known of the malpractice. She's your hero, Mr. and Mrs. Seppala."

We prayed about whether or not to file a malpractice lawsuit and realized that it was the only way to unearth all the details concerning Nancy's medical odyssey, as well as expose the unlawful actions of the hospital staff. In the months to come, our attorneys and the investigators revealed that the pathologist was disgruntled and on the verge of being replaced.

Vows and vision

He believed that this blunder would have blacklisted him in his medical profession for good.

Our hero, the young whistleblower, had jeopardized her job. She was an honest woman, unable to be corrupted, though the pathologist had tried. How much the surgeon actually knew, we'll never discover. The hospital hired big guns (attorneys) to protect themselves and the doctor.

For 27 years, Nancy's one kidney has done its job without a hitch. In this life, we'll never comprehend why we were taken on this stressful journey so soon in our marriage. But we believe that God was positioning us for his purposes. We have learned to accept the suffering in our lives as crucial in the construction of our eternal destinies.

આ આ આ

Our family chose Rindge, New Hampshire, to be our summer hometown. But we needed a house large enough to accommodate the nine of us. When I still owned the 120 acres (called the French Farm), I passed up buying the dilapidated dwelling standing sentry nearby. This original house had been built in 1776 and gazed across the fields like a battered old revolutionary war soldier.

I had often considered what it would take to turn the old house into a habitable home, and one day I brought Nancy to look it over. We scouted the structure from top to bottom. I had my hands full, igniting Nancy's interest in tackling such a challenging construction project. We would need to retain the site's colonial theme, yet create a functional home. She summed up her opinion as we entered the basement. Nancy never left me wondering what she *really* thought.

"The place looks haunted."

The musty smell of centuries-old dirt assaulted our senses as we peered into the bowels of the old soldier. I admired the

The best is yet to come

wooden beams that utterly refused to rot, while Nancy obsessed over a wooden box in a corner.

"That looks like a coffin!"

It was about the size of one, but I knew it was used as a container in the process of butchering hogs.

"Nice home for snakes," she said, wrinkling her nose.

We ascended from the nether regions and cleared our lungs with the fresh air.

"All right, Marty. But you have to fill in that basement and pour concrete over the top." We walked to an old shed attached to the main structure. "And this *has* to go."

I agreed. The two-holer outhouse harked back to an era both of us wanted to forget. I enjoyed watching a total metamorphosis of mind as Nancy's genius emerged. By the time we drove away, she had the old soldier standing in full dress uniform!

After we purchased the lot and started renovations, workers found nary a nail in the whole structure, except a few hand-forged ones upstairs. Every joint in the old sentry had been pegged together with wooden dowels.

We dug a new well, and the water was sweet and clear. Nancy designed a massive living room with a cathedral ceiling, retaining the peg and beam construction. The beams were hand hewn from dense-grained chestnut trees and hard as steel.

We built a great fireplace and installed windows on three sides of the living room. The morning sun lit up the whole house, including the large kitchen with its own popular breakfast nook.

Here I revived my tradition of making blueberry pancakes, and the company never stopped coming. Nancy had our builders turn one of the outbuildings into an apartment with one bedroom, bathroom and a kitchenette. Friends loved our historical "colonial wayfarer's inn."

Each fall we said goodbye to the old soldier and drove south

Vows and vision

to Florida. But sometimes the kindhearted old sentry let a raccoon or two come inside during the cold winters. He even invited one creature to live upstairs until we returned in the spring! The raccoon left his sooty paw prints from the fireplace across the carpet and into the upstairs bedroom.

Long after our children were grown, grandchildren loved to stay at our colonial home. It had a peaceful and healing effect upon our family at times. After our son Ben lost his wife, Kathy, to leukemia, he lived with his children in the main house while Nancy and I used the apartment whenever we traveled to Rindge. After Ben remarried and moved to the West Coast, we put our colonial home on the market, and our old soldier received a new commission.

৵৵৵

Semi-retirement is not all it's cracked up to be, at least not for Marty Seppala. I had gathered all 17 kids for a great powwow and sold all my interest in Seppala & Aho to my boys and girls. At the time, I hoped to receive a monthly salary and balloon payments at the end of each year.

But construction companies all over the country were reeling from the recession, and when my children studied the future, they decided upon drastic changes in S&A. They resolved to shut down the Florida division of the company. My son Jon, who had been in charge of the business there, struck out on his own.

But experience told me that opportunity was ripening again, right in our own backyard. I took Rod Sarkela as a 20 percent partner, and we roared back into the construction business in Florida. We still called ourselves Seppala & Aho, and our completed projects shouted out our good name: Hidden Banyan, Dune Deck, Emeraud, Town Houses at Sloan's Curve, Carlton Place and mid-rise buildings on Hutchinson

The best is yet to come

Island. We could point to the Boynton Beach City Hall as a successful project, too.

The measure of our worth as a company lay in our integrity as Christians, not only in the quality of our products. And once again, God confirmed that he was guiding my decisions. While other businesses struggled to keep afloat, we landed lucrative projects even during the economic upheavals.

Chapter eight
Road to missions

As we kicked off our Florida venture, Rod supervised projects while I beat the brush for more work. One day a business acquaintance, who had bit off more than he could chew, approached me for some help. While razing an old hotel on a beach, his financing on a large construction project had fallen through. He had introduced me to the owners of the property, and after a few meetings, we were close to finalizing a contract.

I sat with George and Stephanie Reibach and their sour-faced attorney in a plush office overlooking the bay, wondering if I had blown the deal out of the water when I voiced concern for their souls at our previous meeting.

"I'm a Christian, and when I die, I am going to heaven. How about you folks?"

George and Stephanie had tactfully changed the subject.

Today I explained the details of my vision for building upscale condominiums. In my proposal, S&A would sell all the units to pay off a bank loan that financed our materials and labor costs. The sales proceeds would also pay the Reibachs for their beachfront property. The bank had agreed to loan S&A several million dollars for construction of a 12-story luxury unit building, if the Reibachs took a *second* position to the bank.

Rod and I needed this contract badly.

"I'd advise against it, Mr. Reibach," his attorney said with raised eyebrows. "It's too great a risk. S&A may not be able to sell the units within an optimal timeframe."

Opportunity hung like ripe oranges, just out of reach. George Reibach stared out the window at cavorting seagulls for

The best is yet to come

a few seconds, obviously mulling over how errant winds in the economy could change fortunes. Suddenly, he turned to me.

"For you, Martin, I'll sign." He nodded decisively at his attorney, who grudgingly handed him the contract.

The Reibachs didn't regret their decision. Rod's construction teams finished Beach Front Condominiums on time, and all the units sold. In the following years, the Seppalas and the Reibachs became more than business associates. We enjoyed a great friendship.

❧❧❧

As I worked in Florida, my "call" to ministry suddenly became solid enough to walk upon. A decade before, a powerful Lutheran pastor had confirmed God's commission for my remaining years of service.

"Martin, I'm an old man. I'd like to pass my mantle to you as minister of the gospel for our Apostolic Lutheran brethren."

This personal blessing from Matti Aho, my childhood pastor, humbled me. I was in my early 50s at the time, and we were traveling together by motor home to Ithaca, New York, for services there. Pastor Matti had known my father and mother well, and his lively messages of salvation had moved many of us boys and girls to confess Jesus as Savior at our New Ipswich church.

My elder and mentor carried in his soul the message of Lutheran revivalists of the 19th century. With his "mantle" on my shoulders, I would embrace an exciting new generation of Apostolic Lutherans who opened their hearts wider to God's grace.

For a season, Pastor Matti's mantle lay in fallow soil, tilled with sorrows and watered by successes. Now, 10 years later, it germinated. I sensed clarity of purpose, and my simple gifts yielded fruit in places I had never dreamed of.

Road to missions

While God expanded the borders of my spiritual territory, our new company flourished in Florida. Nancy and I sponsored a giant pancake breakfast to raise funds for a new church in Lake Worth, along Kirk Road. The growing congregation constructed the building that is still home to Apostolic Lutherans today.

In Florida, an unexpected tide carried me into deeper currents of faith. It seemed that every few days, local families called on me for pastoral duties.

"God's peace, Mr. Seppala. Can you perform our wedding ceremony?"

"Marty, when will you be available to baptize my children?"

"Hey, Martin! Can you stop by and preach at our church?"

At 64 years old, I received no "epiphany," but I felt my soul shift into a higher gear to serve Jesus. As I accepted God's assignments, each new experience became as natural for me as sinking a 16-penny into a Doug fir stud. I felt the confidence and joy of knowing my destiny overflowed, touching people around me. And new doors to ministry were opening.

Among many Lutheran congregations, I was becoming nearly as familiar as their backyard saunas. At conventions, I translated the Finnish language, and Nancy and I were invited to break bread with families after church gatherings. I had employed hundreds of ALC members through the years. Now, in increasing numbers, people from all over the country called me to officiate at their weddings, baptize babies and converts and preach the word of God.

Our youngest children had flown the coop to start families, and grandchildren were popping up on both East and West Coasts with regularity. Sam was doing well in his business in New Hampshire, and Rod had the Florida division well in hand.

While busily serving God and running S&A, Nancy and I barely noticed the immense cultural shift taking place in the world around us. While we built S&A with Rod, our Apostolic

The best is yet to come

Lutheran Church members in Finland hailed the approaching collapse of the communist government in the U.S.S.R.

President Ronald Reagan had challenged the Soviets with the words, "Tear down this wall!" in front of Germany's Brandenburg Gate. By the end of 1989, the Berlin Wall between Soviet-controlled East Germany and free West Germany had been dismantled. The Soviet Union itself began dissolving into separate republics. Our Finnish brethren in the districts around Leningrad (now called Saint Petersburg) savored the first taste of religious freedom in half a century.

In 1990, Finnish Pastor Kurt Snellman invited Nancy and me to join a mission trip to the U.S.S.R. We visited ALC congregations in Finland before traveling by bus across the Finnish/Soviet border. This was the first of six visits I made to Russia, including two trips with family members to help with the adoptions of six Russian children.

The Cold War still simmered during our first missionary trip into the U.S.S.R. At the border, unfriendly Soviet officials studied Nancy's and my American passports, while ordering our driver to park the tour bus over a trench to inspect its underbelly. Nancy and I were shunted aside while guards herded our Finnish companions through checkpoints. Most of the 50 missionaries carried tape recorders and cameras, and some were confiscated. While officials examined the interior of the bus, Nancy and I were cleared to join Pastor Snellman and our friends.

Our destination was Finnish communities around Leningrad, on the Karelian Isthmus. Most of us had stuffed our luggage with tapes of sermons to give to brethren living behind the Iron Curtain.

Altogether we carried 1,000 Bibles with handwritten greetings inside each one: "God's grace and peace be with you, from the Finnish people of New Ipswich, Ashburnham and Hockinson congregations."

Road to missions

At the end of World War II, Finland had agreed to cede the Karelian Isthmus to the U.S.S.R. as part of reparations (punishment) for Finland's military alliance with Germany. Thousands of Finns fled the Isthmus, but multiple thousands were trapped by Soviet troops or chose to remain with their farms and businesses.

The Soviets had immediately demolished or closed Finnish Lutheran churches and schools. The secret police outlawed Finnish publications and radio broadcasts throughout the region. The Soviet military murdered tens of thousands of Finnish men or sent them to Siberian work camps.

Leadership in Moscow still described Finnish people as "politically unreliable." While suffering oppression for 50 years, the Soviet Finns still doggedly clung to their culture and language to pass on to the next generation.

After the dismantling of the Berlin wall, Finnish Christians had sensed a slight loosening in the yoke of religious oppression for the first time. Leaders in the Apostolic Lutheran Church immediately asked the Soviet Union for approval to entertain missionaries in their Finnish communities. We were some of the first missionaries "authorized" by the government to personally encourage our Finnish brethren on the Karelian Isthmus.

We traveled through territory that some in our number remembered as part of their homeland. They recalled when the Soviets gained control of the region and secret police destroyed every Bible they could find.

We tried not to make eye contact with the Soviet soldiers cradling machine guns on street corners. We unloaded at a hotel in Leningrad and immediately drove to hold our first church service at a suburb outside the city. In a building that accommodated about 100 people, no more seats were available, so several in the congregation stood in the back. They hadn't heard a Finnish sermon in many years.

The best is yet to come

"Where are all the elders?" I asked a woman with teary blue eyes. She looked to be about my own age. It seemed that widows outnumbered everyone else.

"Siberia, Pastor Seppala. The police stole our Finnish boys and men years ago. Some say they were taken to work camps. Others say they were killed. We don't know ..."

In this woman's face, hardships were etched in every wrinkle. "And you have no church to worship in?" I asked.

"*Our* churches have been cemeteries. Sometimes vacant buildings, like this. Or our homes, of course." She shrugged with a resigned smile.

In some communities, my Finnish brethren lived in houses with dirt floors and had barely enough food to feed their families. A black market thrived in meat and vodka. Thieves watched for unattended cars, and our drivers unfastened windshield wipers to lock them out of sight. Cabbage was the staple in a Soviet citizen's diet: coleslaw, soups and desserts.

One evening we were due to preach at 7 p.m., and I felt irritated at being late for the service. Our bus trundled down dirt roads to collect folks for the meeting, and we struggled through traffic jams. Finally we arrived at our destination, three hours late!

At the bombed-out building where we were scheduled to speak, I glanced at my watch. "Nancy, I wonder if anyone will be inside ..."

She held up her hand. "Listen!"

Voices of praise drifted across the street, inviting a smile to our lips. We hurried upstairs to a cold, rickety balcony, and inside, a group of about 75 people greeted me like Paul the Apostle! They had been worshiping Jesus for three hours, seated on hard benches, waiting. At 10 p.m., three of us began speaking the word of God in Finnish, which was translated into Russian, and no one fell asleep. We preached long past midnight.

Road to missions

Congregations were so unlike those in the States. No one flipped pages in their Bibles, reading scripture verses along with me. They left their Bibles at home, hidden away in a safe place.

After the service, Nancy took me aside. "Have you been in the bathroom?"

I shook my head. "You need to go see ..." she said quietly.

I excused myself and found the lavatory: a single grimy hole in the floor. One risked falling in, if you were desperate enough to use it.

I had lived with every comfort imaginable: fine meals daily, plenty of money from a thriving business, splendid church buildings, swimming pools, saunas and luxury cars. Above all, I enjoyed the freedom to raise my family in the nurture and admonition of God. As I spoke to my oppressed brethren in the Soviet Union, God awakened in me the ambition to serve forsaken and impoverished people with my resources and knowledge. I prayed for God to show me where and how.

To those under communism, the gospel of Jesus Christ slams hard against a lifetime of atheist indoctrination. Nancy spoke to a young woman named Sonja about her eternal destiny. She was assigned as our tour guide. Sonia had a background in the Russian Orthodox religion.

Speaking of her nation's religious heritage, she said, "It's all tradition that has no meaning."

Nancy didn't press the girl to make a commitment to Christ that she didn't understand. Instead, she asked her to pray that God would reveal the truth about Jesus to her, so she could be saved.

"But I don't know any prayers," Sonja said, seriously.

"Just ask Jesus to show himself to your heart, Sonja."

This was the first time this girl had heard God's word spoken by a Christian.

Tenderhearted friends in foreign countries are hungry for God. In our travels, we have learned to put our faith in Jesus to

The best is yet to come

do the work of conversion, rather than browbeat people into making decisions before they are ready.

I left the U.S.S.R. promising that I would pray for my brethren and someday return to preach the word again. I left fear behind on the Soviet side of the border. In Finland, no soldiers glared at me from street corners. Upon returning home to the United States, I treasured freedom like never before.

The Cold War between the United States and the Soviet Union ended a year after we visited the Finnish enclaves around Leningrad. In 1991, reformers entered the Russian government, and Christians cautiously emerged from the shadows, carrying their Bibles in plain view. Apostolic Lutheran brethren in the new "Russian Federation" pooled their meager resources to build churches, and Finns all over America and Finland chipped in.

Our hosts on the Karelian Isthmus invited me back to help dedicate one of the churches now legally sanctioned by the Russian government. Nancy tended business at home while I crossed the Finland/Russia border again. Guards checked my passport and luggage, absent the suspicion Nancy and I had experienced the year before. I accompanied a missionary group to Saint Petersburg, a new name for the city formerly called Leningrad.

I'll never forget the more than 500 tearful Lutheran Christians who gathered at a thanksgiving dedication service celebrating one of the first churches to be reconstructed in 50 years. I was privileged to openly preach the gospel in the Finnish language, translated into Russian.

One excited 16-year-old boy, named Simo, asked the principal of his school if we could preach there, and she graciously invited us to address three classes. No principal in our own government-run schools would have allowed us to come. As I met the school staff, I noticed a glaring absence of men, and it gave me pause. Women carried the burden of many important positions in Russian society due to a high rate of alcoholism among men.

A question from one Russian boy revealed the distorted picture of Americans that had been painted by the old Soviet regime. "Did you bring your guns with you today?" he asked. Many of these students expected Americans to be gun-toting, hateful extremists. I told him that I didn't even own a gun, and neither did any of my brothers.

I came home weary but renewed in my spirit. At 65 years old, with Nancy at my side, I felt as ambitious and challenged as I had been at 20. In time, I would return to assist missionaries living on the frontlines in foreign countries, but for now, God was opening doors to ministry right where I lived.

꽃꽃꽃

My checks from the sale of S&A to my children stopped coming from the Northeast around 1991. The New Ipswich-based company had produced income for me like clockwork for decades, and suddenly I was starting from scratch again. A regional recession emptied the Northeast of construction work, and businesses stopped expanding. Only smaller construction projects appeared on the horizon, so my second to oldest son, Sam, wisely downsized to survive. My family closed the New Ipswich office for good, selling off assets and settling accounts.

Four million dollars owed to S&A "evaporated" in this recession, as few of our accounts had funds to pay off their debts to us. By God's grace, the Florida-based construction company had been rolling along nicely under Rod's management, and I cogitated on expanding into a new area, with a fresh agenda. The time seemed ripe for offering affordable quality housing to families. At the time, banks were making it easy for people to finance a new home.

I planned to assemble a team of builders to mass-produce

The best is yet to come

housing, and all we needed was *land* in a solid working-class demographic. After a scouting trip, Nancy put the kibosh on Virginia. She studied the area and decided that demand for the number of homes we anticipated building would likely fall flat. But when I explored South Carolina, I found land to be inexpensive and available to produce homes by the hundreds. High taxes and out-of-control bureaucracies had not yet strangled business growth or potential employment in the South.

We opened a new S&A company based near Greenville, South Carolina. From a rented apartment, Nancy and I designed basic floor plans and began inviting our kids to help launch a fresh Christ-centered commercial enterprise. Our vision began to take shape when my son Amos and his wife, Jana, moved to Greenville. Cliff and Nancy's daughter Janie agreed to come aboard. Later my boy Josh and Nancy's daughter Alice came, too. Finally, Benji and Nancy's daughter Norma threw in with us as well. We all broke ground together in our new venture. With sacrifice and dedication, our kids invested their sweat and money into a lucrative project that lasted for a decade.

This adventure turned into a solid, ongoing ministry as well. No Finns had ever planted an Apostolic Lutheran Church in Greenville County, so I felt God's nudge to plow new spiritual ground and plant seeds in our neighborhood. Our congregation of family and a few neighbors immediately met for Sunday services, and the kids performed our first Christmas program at the Cavalier Woods Apartments at Mauldin, a town outside of Greenville.

My business model has always been to test the market and, if successful, dive in head first. In the beginning, we purchased a couple lots, then grabbed hammers and levels to build one affordable spec home in a subdivision called Chick Springs. Nancy shepherded our first sale to completion, and we all breathed a little easier, knowing we could pay the bills with our proceeds.

Feeling confident that other homes would sell in Chick Springs, we bought up other lots and built as fast as our crews could erect walls to our slabs. Slab-on-grade construction struck Southern builders as a "strange" idea. They built homes the way their daddies did: with a crawlspace underneath their houses or a basement. After we had sold a few homes modeled after our plans, folks got used to the idea, and the Southern builders followed in our footsteps.

We called our company Seppala & Aho in South Carolina. When Josh and Alice moved into the fourth house in the subdivision to show it. Nancy and I started looking for other land around Greer, not far from Greenville. A city building inspector told me about Maplewood, a failed project that the owner wanted to unload. The city needed the subdivision completed, and we had the reputation for prompt quality construction. Greer public works met with me, and city officials offered to run all the water and sewer lines without charge. S&A bought the whole kit and caboodle.

Nancy and I planted a big project trailer on a lot at the subdivision and moved in to supervise the construction progress. We managed about 50 lots. Ten homes were already occupied in this old subdivision. Nancy showed homes night and day. We began advertising, and customers made down payments before many of the houses were even built. Families loved Nancy's floor plans. We built most of the houses with very open designs and cathedral ceilings. We assigned each floor plan names according to size and quality: King, Queen, Princess, Duchess and Monarch.

Looking back on our Maplewood project, I recall only one hiccup. I directed a brush-clearing operation smack dab in the middle of the subdivision. I obtained a legal burn permit, and we bulldozed the acreage, piling the slash into big mounds. We tried to incinerate the debris, but it burned way too slowly for me. It held up our momentum. This was wild country, with water moccasins, hornets and spiders hiding in the woods everywhere.

I rented a high-output air blower to speed things along and attached a pipe to feed air beneath the piles to super-heat the slash. It worked like a charm for one day. But the next morning a heavy buildup of ash plugged the pipe hole. The blower huffed and puffed, like it was blowing up a big air balloon.

"Swing that bucket, and clear away the ash!" I hollered at the backhoe operator, and he looked a little doubtful as I pantomimed my orders over the blower's roar.

He got the message and did exactly as I told him. Ash suddenly exploded into a gray plume above the pipe hole. Hot ash kept spewing 100 feet into the air where the gentle southern breezes carried it across Maplewood Subdivision onto rooftops, windowsills, cars and sidewalks. Swimming pools turned gray, and ash clogged air-conditioning filters.

Just before the first customer rapped on our job trailer, the backhoe operator, wide-eyed, informed me, "Marty, it's raining!"

Streaks of gray grit ran down the sides of our job trailer, and I could only imagine what our customers' homes looked like.

Nancy's public relations skills quelled the riot of angry homeowners. We had to compensate a good many for cleanups and carwashes. We chipped up the rest of the slash piles, a horribly tiresome process. The fire department revoked our burn permit, and the city kicked us out of the job trailer. We moved into one of the houses before it sold.

However, for the most part, we had a great relationship with the building department. We kept them informed of how many bedrooms and bathrooms each of our 50 houses had. They issued us permits as we detailed the square footage and sales values. Inspectors came and went, giving approval after each construction phase.

As business increased, we rented office space on Highway 14, near the airport, and hired bookkeepers to keep our accounting up to par. Volume increased, and S&A purchased a house and had it rezoned for "business." It became our permanent office.

The growth of our "family church" kept pace with our business success. We decided to build a place to fellowship, so Nancy and I purchased a lot on Rutherford Road in Greer, then donated it to our tenacious, loving congregation. Over a three-year period, the congregation had outgrown our apartment. We then met at Josh's spacious home for a time. Soon we had to meet at the Lion's Club in Greer, but burst out of the seams there, too. Dozens of former employees and friends from across the country joined our S&A workforce. Experienced Finnish laborers, carpenters, electricians, masons and sales personnel (with all their wives and children) now filled our gatherings.

For a time, we met at an old vacuum cleaner store, but soon realized that our congregation needed more room again! Nancy and an architect designed plans to build our new church on the lot on Rutherford Road. We utilized our pool of Finnish construction men to build the first Apostolic Lutheran Church in Greenville County, South Carolina.

As the congregation gained membership, Doug Coponen and Wayne Kinnunen moved close by to assist me in preaching the word of God. Over the years, we added a spacious kitchen and fellowship hall to the main building. At more than 300 people, we were outgrowing these facilities as well and voted to plant a whole new church, rather than build on again.

During these busy years in Greer, one of my plumbers came to the office after work. "Martin, I need some help." He seemed embarrassed as he continued. "My son is in jail. Can you go talk to him?"

The best is yet to come

It was the first time I had visited the Greenville Detention Center, a stark, over-lit building with unemotional, solemn-faced men in uniforms watching everyone carefully. The guards dutifully escorted downcast inmates to booths with chairs on either side of bulletproof glass. Inmates and visitors directed their voices through a hole in the glass, a little smaller than a fist.

I spoke with the young man for an allotted time of 30 minutes, encouraging him to give his life to Jesus, but left with a heavy heart. How could a person live for months or years without family near or the freedom to make decisions for himself? Only God's grace could save a man or woman from depression or inner rage when deprived of basic human freedoms, whether caused by his or her own actions or by living in a police state like Russia.

I realized that the incarcerated in Greenville and my Russian friends overseas faced a common evil force seeking to control their destinies. Knowing their sense of hopelessness and abandonment fired up a desire to show them God's way of peace. The fields were "white unto harvest," right in my own backyard.

I took a training course from the State of South Carolina required for pastoral prison visitation. After my reception and evaluation process, the prison system sanctioned me to visit prisoners at the Greenville Correctional Center and the Perry County Correctional Center at Pelzer. I met with up to 50 inmates at a time to share the gospel. This was the beginning of my ministry in several prisons in the United States and three prisons in Russia. During the 10 years I worked and ministered in South Carolina, I met with inmates weekly.

I recall one man, a former drug dealer tormented by his past, who asked me, "Is there any help for me?"

I told him about Jesus, whose blood could erase his guilt and insure his eternal destiny the instant he believed and trusted him to forgive his sins. Behind bars, even after a true conversion to Christ, a man or woman faces memories that torment him or her during hours of silent reflection. As it is on the outside of prison, Bible studies, prayer meetings and fellowship become the life blood of incarcerated believers. I encouraged others to preach and speak with these precious redeemed souls.

God continued to bless our Greer church, as well as our business endeavors. In time, Josh and Amos decided to break away to start their own contracting companies, and I bought them out. Cliff Somero and Benji Reini bought in and helped me manage the growth of S&A in South Carolina. Although smaller than the multiple expansions of our heyday 25 years before, our payroll continued to grow.

Over the decades as an employer, I prayed often for the safety of my employees. At one time, I had more than 600 men and women on the S&A payrolls. To head off accidents, we called for safety meetings regularly. By God's grace, Seppala & Aho experienced relatively few serious accidents in my 45 years in business.

In the 1980s, I hired Ted Seppala to enforce safe practices on the job, and the number of work-related accidents plummeted dramatically. Our insurance rate dropped by $100,000 per year, a sizeable sum in those days.

A crane was the evil specter in nearly all of our fatal accidents.

Once, while a young man was holding the heavy iron boom, electricity jumped eight feet from a nearby high-voltage wire and traveled down the cable, killing him instantly. Another time a crane cable snapped, and the boom landed on top of a man. The third fatality involved a man standing too close to the counterweight behind the crane. It shoved him into the path of the boom.

A crane was absent in only one fatal circumstance. It

The best is yet to come

happened in Vermont, where a gust of wind blew down a section of steel and crushed a man.

Like thousands in the construction trades, these men risked their lives as members of our American workforce. They are distinguished and remembered as integral parts of the most innovative army of workers in history. With their families, I grieve over the loss of each one.

~~~

At 74 years old, I spent three weeks visiting prisons in Russia with a small team of ALC pastors, including Bruce Selin and Greg Helmes. Dennis Hilman was a resident missionary in a small Russian town called Yakenturnburg, in a jasper mining district. The oppressive atmosphere in Russia had lifted considerably after the end of the Cold War, and soldiers no longer guarded streets wherever we traveled. Pastor Dennis had a congregation of about 100, and we slept at his home.

Our first prison held incarcerated 13- to 19-year-old boys, and we met in a room that accommodated about 16 of these children at a time. The four of us men preached with the same theme in mind: "Remember your Creator in the days of your youth ..."

We spoke about how much the Savior loved them, and the Holy Spirit grabbed hold of these children. Tears ran down their dirty cheeks. It was as if they had been *waiting* for someone to tell them the way of salvation. They confessed their sins in the name of Jesus and by the power of his precious blood, and we confirmed to each one that, truly, their sins were forgiven.

The boys shuffled off to their rooms with joy written on their faces. The next group entered, a little tentative. Some were surly, some fearful, but as soon as we showed them God's love, they reached out to us with the same desperation, seeking God's cleansing in their hearts, too. I'll never forget the tears of remorse and sheer relief on their faces, as they left to make room for the next group.

For each of these children, it wasn't enough to hear the message of the gospel. These boys wanted to *know* that their sins were completely erased in God's book. It was such a privilege to pronounce God's peace upon them, declaring their freedom from sin. Amazingly, the third group reacted the same way as the first two, with the Holy Spirit healing their young hearts.

Pastor Dennis diligently took down the names of these boys. Several looked him up after their prison terms were over.

The guards at the prison were mostly women, very rough-cut individuals. After the third group of boys left the room, a female guard marched up to inform us that we must leave immediately. She was disturbed at how these boys reacted after their "religious" experiences. She glared after us with resentment.

Dennis, who spoke Russian fluently and translated for us, secured other engagements at prisons, including one "experimental" one. Unlike the prison for boys, these inmates were grown men, hardened by prison. We spoke to about 50 men gathered in a designated hall. Dressed in spanking clean uniforms, they had jobs working in state-provided vegetable gardens or carpentry shops. According to officials who spoke with us, the recidivism rate, due to this "relaxed" atmosphere, was much lower here than for other Russian prisons.

Unlike the lads who rushed to Jesus for forgiveness, these men sat politely, unmoved. Overall, they were contented with their lives and showed little remorse for their past crimes.

"Let us sing for you!"

They seemed to think that their vocal performances satisfied God and his requirement for "religion" in their lives.

The contrast between the two age groups reaffirmed my

The best is yet to come

lifelong belief that we must reach men and women with the salvation message while they are tenderhearted, at a young age. A heart grows more and more calloused toward the gospel the longer one lives as an unbeliever.

A prison with 7,000 inmates sprawls in an unpopulated region about 100 miles from Yakenturnburg. We chose to visit girls there who were raising their babies in the Russian prison system. Fifty of the 70 young women came to our service. My short sermon came from John 3:16, and I told how God had lavished his love upon them and that all they needed to do was confess their sins and believe in Jesus to have eternal life. Most of these girls were kids in their teens.

Through my translator I ended my sermon with, "Children, pray to God and say, 'If you are real, reveal yourself unto me! I want to live forever and worship you and believe in you.'"

A Russian girl, about 18 years old, interrupted me. "You are a good man! Can't we pray to you?"

After Dennis translated this for me, I stood for a few seconds, shocked by this young woman's childlike innocence. She would be easily led by anyone who showed love to her.

"You must never pray to any human. You must only pray to God, the Creator of the whole world," I told her gently.

After the service, the girls gathered around us. "Come see our babies. You must see our little ones!"

They had dressed their infants in brightly colored clothing they made in prison from cloth donated by Pastor Dennis. I took a group picture and promised to send them copies.

Siberia was our next destination, to visit a Finnish community in the suburbs of a city called Novosibirsk. We traveled nearly 3,000 miles by train in a Pullman car, then lodged at an upscale hotel among high-rises and factories. With more than a million people, Novosibirsk is the largest city in Siberia.

We met with Finnish-speaking congregations who

welcomed us with the Finnish Lutheran greeting: "God's peace!"

These people spoke the same Old Finnish dialect as I, and I comfortably translated for my companions. It was a sad time leaving these beautiful souls, mostly elderly. I wondered who would carry on the Finnish Apostolic Lutheran traditions when they were gone.

We rode the train to Moscow and flew home, leaving Dennis to carry on the hard work as an Apostolic Lutheran missionary in a land of political upheavals and uncertain freedoms.

త్తిత్తిత్తి

I embraced my seventh decade of life, still being shaped by the new experiences God had in store. My family life has schooled me in patience and love. My work in commercial enterprises trained me to accept challenges and persevere in the face of trials. Through mission travels, God was showing me his blueprint for expanding his kingdom.

Working in Finland, Norway, Sweden, Russia, Guatemala, Sri Lanka, India and Myanmar has deepened my desire to be part of Jesus' plan, which includes men and women in every hemisphere. On a trip to Guatemala City, I preached in several churches, as well as an orphanage. My missionary friends, Edgar and Lizzette Franco, introduced me to Lizzette's brother, a professor in Guatemala.

As he showed me his extensive library, I noticed that most volumes bore theological names. I asked, "Have you read all of these?"

"Most of them," he said.

"And what is your final conclusion, after studying what these authors have to say?"

He paused a moment and took off his glasses. His dark eyes

danced as he said, "Jesus loves me, this I know. For the Bible tells me so ..."

I am still amazed how the Holy Spirit summarizes the greatest commentaries ever written in a simple Sunday school song.

ॐॐॐ

I celebrated my 80th birthday while on a mission trip in Sri Lanka. I flew to this poor, densely-populated country with a leader in our ALC foreign mission effort, Pastor Bob Maki. My two sons Amos and Matthew also traveled with me, along with Randy Questad. He had spearheaded collections from individuals in the United States to purchase Sri Lanka Pastor Lynton Sylva's house.

We stayed at a small motel near Pastor Lynton's home. He and his wife, Iona, have been missionaries sponsored by our churches in the United States for many years. Pastor Lynton's remodeled "sanctuary" garage resounds with God's praise every Sunday. During the week, he drives his van to various trailheads, sometimes loaded with clothing to give to needy villagers. Most of Sri Lanka's population is Buddhist or minority Hindu — bitter, bloody enemies in recent years.

Pastor Lynton's pastoral duties include hiking to remote areas to preach about Jesus, the Way, the Truth and the Life. We followed him (sometimes miles) into these communities while a blend of jungle voices screeched all around us. Red-faced macaques and black-faced langur monkeys swung in the treetops above us. On the narrow, well-worn paths to villages, the thick green foliage hid the squalor of Sri Lankans until we burst into clearings where residents lived in huts.

A family of four lived inside a single mud-block building about the size of a large chicken coop. Parents slept with their children side-by-side, upon hard-dried beds of mud, raised above the floors. We arrived to visit one family, and the homemaker seemed put out about us arriving unexpectedly. She made it clear we couldn't go inside.

Pastor Lynton reassured her and explained to me, "She just spread mud for her floor. It hasn't hardened yet, so we'll talk to the family *outside* today." The woman's face reminded me of Nancy's warning glare when she had just cleaned and waxed her kitchen floors at home.

A new believer in Christ within a community of traditional Buddhists is shunned; the visits they receive from Pastor Lynton are their only Christian fellowship. I had wonderful communion with families, singing with them and sharing God's word. In these mud shanties, I'll never forget the welcoming smiles and genuine sorrow at our departure.

On this mission trip to Asia, God's love touched me powerfully as I reflected upon the poor living conditions of my brothers and sisters in Christ. They didn't covet worldly goods They treasured the little they possessed and gloried in a relationship with Jesus that filled all voids.

At a hospital, we prayed for a man nearly killed in one of the myriad vehicle collisions on the muddy streets. In the one big room with dozens of beds, we also met a young logger who supported three families with his wages. A massive landslide had ripped his leg loose from joints around his groin. His condition haunted me after we left the hospital.

He was a working man, like my boys and me. Could he survive infections in this primitive infirmary? All we could do was pray that God blessed him with the faith to believe in Jesus. His eternal destiny was likely close at hand.

All my life, I have been entrusted with ambition, physical strength and freedom to pursue my dreams. To understand these people, I had to stretch spiritual muscles I had never before used. My Jesus was changing my heart, humbling me as I embraced these wonderful Christians abroad.

The best is yet to come

We traveled into the tea-producing areas of Sri Lanka where hundreds of people picked the leaves for major companies. Along the sides of the roads, women sat with small hammers, beating on fist-sized rocks, turning them into crushed gravel.

Pastor Lynton explained, "Men here use handheld drills and sledge hammers to break rocks into chunks. Then our women break them down to gravel-size, to spread as road base."

Like always, I jumped at a chance to improve their effectiveness: with bulldozers, dump trucks, loaders …

"Why doesn't the government bring in heavy equipment?" I asked.

Pastor Lynton smiled patiently. "Marty, women are paid about a dollar a day to break rocks. For many, this is their only means of supporting their families. The government knows this and keeps the poor people of our country working."

Before we flew off to India to continue our Asia itinerary, we purchased a welding machine and a concrete block-forming machine for Pastor Lynton to use as he saw fit.

�����

In India, thousands of bicycles and motorcycles competed for the right-of-way on busy city thoroughfares. Caricatures of public transportation hauled more people on the outside of their frames than inside. These buses could easily have been recruited in Disneyland or Magic Mountain for comic thrill rides. I watched a family of five attach themselves to a motorcycle for a jaunt across town. "Truckers" fastened 4-foot stacks of wood to unwieldy bicycle racks.

In a city about 100 miles from Chennai, India, called Rajahmundry, we visited Dr. Syam Kumar, an Indian national who has organized an Apostolic Lutheran outreach program of more than 100 ALC congregations. At Dr. Kumar's two-story

Road to missions

hospital, up to 300 people per day are treated without charge.

Donations from Christians, like the Alvar Helmes family, have kept the doors open for years. Nancy and I were able to donate an x-ray machine and ultrasound equipment. We also donated funds for a printing press that has produced more than one million copies of the booklet *Follow Jesus and Prevent AIDS.* It has been translated into several languages and changed thousands of lives.

In several meetings a day, with groups ranging from three to 900 people at homes, orphanages, open-air meetings and in giant tents, our little contingent of Finnish preachers had our hands full. Dr. Kumar was gracious and informative as to the reason these people were so receptive. In the previous century, the blood of Christian martyrs had shed love and light upon India. He told of a missionary woman who had left her husband to raise money in the States. She waited for him to arrive later. When he never came home, she returned to the Indian village where they had ministered together.

Her husband's body hung on a pole at the village gate, a warning to any who dared carry the Christian gospel into their community again. Nevertheless, this woman made her home in the same village, winning over Hindus by her courage and unreserved forgiveness.

We traveled to an island, and Dr. Kumar explained on the trip that the inhabitants never used to come to the mainland. The boat that carried us had been constructed from plans used for generations. It was built like a long canoe, and a man stood in the stern stroking a long pole back and forth to move the craft forward.

Years before, the first missionary to this island had been murdered by the islanders. But more Apostolic Lutheran missionaries dared to follow in his footsteps. Now we were welcomed to a great meeting at the shore. The islanders were praising God.

The best is yet to come

I believe I sampled the same fulfillment as Paul the Apostle experienced on his missionary journeys. Like him, my companions and I encouraged believers living under difficult conditions. We also held mission meetings geared for the unsaved. At one of these gatherings, 900 people sat on towels or rugs in the dirt, spilling far beyond the tent that had been erected.

At this meeting, Bob Maki and I carried the gospel message. We threw open the tent flaps and prayed that our sound equipment would carry our voices to the ones straining to hear. Our hosts faced the same dilemma as Jesus and his disciples: feeding the masses that needed to hear the good news of salvation. Our loving hosts spread plastic on the ground behind the tent, then piled huge mounds of cooked rice and chicken on these plastic "platters."

We were exhausted after preaching for so many hours, and the people mobbed us, hungry for God's touch through his ambassadors. Hundreds crowded the stage. Brown hands clutched at our arms, pulling us to them, placing our hands on their heads.

Their sweet voices cried out, "Bless me! Bless me!"

It was impossible to reach every one. We could only offer a prayer of blessing for them en mass. After their evening meal, they asked us to preach all over again, but we were worn to the nubs! The local pastor asked us to come again.

"Next time we'll have a much larger crowd, Martin. And we'll set up tent services like this one!"

❧❧❧❧

The last stop on our Asian mission tour was in Myanmar, a nation known for its despotic government. Christians are considered outlaws in Myanmar, and we were warned not to bow our heads to pray in public or speak to the nationals about

Road to missions

Jesus openly. The ALC leadership who cared for our needs were of Chinese descent. Their base of operations was a building known in their community as a clothes tailoring school. Along with learning to use sewing machines, the students clandestinely studied the Bible.

We preached at the homes of impoverished Christians in communities with elegant 100-acre Buddhist temple sanctuaries maintained by hundreds of dedicated monks. The temple exteriors exuded outrageous wealth, with gold-plated siding and inlaid gems decorating the walls. Stone statues of Buddha dominated the cities in one of the poorest nations on earth. Monks busied themselves begging for money everywhere to support these great monuments to darkness.

The faithful men and women of Myanmar never took for granted "God's peace." They laid their lives on the line whenever they gathered in the name of Jesus. I left this country with a renewed commitment to lovingly exhort my friends in America to treasure every moment they sang praises to Jesus' name without fear of reprisal.

Chapter nine
A thoroughly lived life

In 1888, my grandfather and great-grandparents disembarked in New York to start their new lives in America. Forty-six years later, in 1934, I braced for my first elevator ride with my father, Gus Seppala, in a New York high-rise hotel. Seeing them from my 8-year-old vantage point, New York's mighty structures of concrete and steel stirred my ambition to think "big." Since then, I've navigated the crowded freeways of New York many times.

On September 11, 2001, Nancy and I sat speechless as we watched planes, controlled by al-Qaeda terrorists, strike New York's World Trade Center. On our television, the Twin Towers (along with our sense of national security) crumbled before our eyes. Another airliner struck the Pentagon in Virginia.

Hijacked United Airlines Flight 93 was en route to Washington, D.C. — the supposed target, the White House. Brave passengers fought the terrorists for control of Flight 93, but it crashed in a reclaimed coal strip mine near Shanksville, Pennsylvania.

The administration of President George. W. Bush immediately announced a "War on Terror" to prevent the growth of al-Qaeda networks.

I was 17 when U.S. troops recaptured Guadalcanal. I was 18 when our boys fought the bloody Battle of the Bulge. World War II and its effects on my family are branded upon most of my boyhood memories. In my lifetime, I have witnessed war with Germany, war with Japan, wars in Finland, the Korean War, the Vietnam War, the Cold War, the War in Iraq, a war in

A thoroughly lived life

Afghanistan and an escalating global war with militant Muslim extremists.

On missionary adventures, I have met Christians in countries governed by dictators, parliaments, military despots, communists and socialists. None of these governments favorably compare to our free American democratic republic. I'm convinced, as never before, that widening international conflicts are part of the "birth pangs" Jesus has described in his word. He said plainly that "wars and rumors of wars" would precede his return (Matthew 24:6).

In May of 1948, just days before I married my first wife, Barbara, the United States recognized the new State of Israel as a sovereign nation. I was 22 then and too absorbed with my wedding to appreciate the prophetic magnitude of this event. Nearly 2,500 years earlier, God had promised, through the prophet Amos, that he would "plant Israel in their own land, never again to be uprooted ..." (Amos 9:14-15).

While I was busy rearing 17 children and establishing Seppala & Aho, Jews from every corner of the earth returned to their Promised Land. Today Israel is the corner stake driven deeply into history from which we survey the future. God promises blessings or curses based upon a nation's treatment of his chosen people, the Jews.

Nancy and I visited Israel in 1999 with a company of Finnish travelers. On our tour, we explored all the familiar Biblical addresses, like the Garden of Gethsemane, the Via Delarosa and the Mount of Olives. On a level beneath the narrations and tours, the Holy Spirit affirmed to me that Jesus' homecoming was *closer than ever*. I sensed God's sovereign hand upon the Jewish people, despite their open rejection of the Messiah's first advent.

Israel's nationalistic government has always restricted non-Jewish entrepreneurs from purchasing or leasing property to grow businesses. But in 1971, they made an exception.

The best is yet to come

A group of investors asked the Israeli government for land to build a Moshav (settlement) called Yad Hashmona (Memorial for the Eight). This contingent of Finnish Christians hoped to establish a memorial of forgiveness for a particular human rights crime committed during World War II. Finland had handed over eight Jews to the Nazi Gestapo, in compliance with Hitler's Final Solution.

In 1971, the Israeli government granted these Finnish Lutherans permission to build Yad Hoshmona, just outside of historic Jerusalem. We Finns now celebrate the memorial as a tribute to Israel's role in Christianity.

Our Finnish tour group stayed at the motel in Yad Hashmona, and I was privileged to speak with one of its tenacious Christian founders.

In 1970, he had approached the "suspicious" Israeli government to explain his dream of building a memorial of forgiveness in the Judean hills for the world to experience. No one in the Jewish bureaucracy would listen at first, but his Nordic resolve finally paid off.

"After I talked to Golda Meir, she bent the rules for us," the balding elder wryly told me. He pointed to a sign at the entrance of the complex and read it aloud: "The Return of the Eight!"

Today, about 150 people live at Yad Hashmona: families, singles, children, volunteers and students of the Israel Bible Extension project. A Jewish man who runs the Moshav said that the Finnish people planted kindness in Israel.

"We Jews fight, fight, fight all the time. You Finns have taught us how to forgive," he said.

In this world of greed and strife, I'm humbled to convey the Apostolic Lutheran greeting "God's peace" to people wherever I have traveled. For me, "God's peace" expresses to unseen forces of angels and demons my personal conviction that God is ultimately in control of this earth.

A thoroughly lived life

And the phrase also reminds me of a blessed morning when I shall awaken to *see* the Prince of Peace.

જ⋅જ⋅જ

Nancy and I had been moving toward a busy, efficient life of semi-retirement and ministry when out of the blue a man from National Homes Inc. approached me.

He carried a gold-plated "monkey wrench."

"Would you consider selling Seppala & Aho in South Carolina?"

I chuckled. "No, sir. I'm not interested."

I was about to end the conversation when he asked, "What if we offered you $14 million? Would you discuss the possibility then?"

The figure sparked my curiosity, but I kept my voice noncommittal. "I'll run it by my partners," I said.

Nancy and I kicked the "possibility" around for a few days. We were at the top of our game, clearing about $4 million that year before taxes. We contemplated the many ways we could bless and strengthen missionary work if we held onto S&A.

But, perhaps the time was *right* to sell …

Cliff, Janie, Benji and Norma had a stake in the company, so we talked to them about selling as well. We came to the decision to test the waters.

National Homes Inc. had a fine reputation and seemed financially solid, so we moved forward to sell S&A in South Carolina. NHI agreed to allow our employees to stay on, and Nancy and I planned to be involved in managing some phases of their construction projects. Through months of negotiations, our lawyers and theirs hammered out the details. We happily signed contracts and anticipated a friendly partnership with NHI. Then our plans struck a knot.

Behind the scenes, another corporation called Gypco Inc.

The best is yet to come

had acquired NHI and all their subsidiaries. We found ourselves dealing with a company that had no intentions of honoring the good-faith arrangements we expected from NHI. Only the basic tenets of our contract were acknowledged. Gypco laid off most of our honest, experienced employees and replaced them with their own. At the same time, we were still under contract with Gypco to provide our expertise in land acquisitions and some construction services.

Nancy and I created a new company called Martin Henry Investments, and Josh partnered with us to help manage it. We promised to acquire land around South Carolina for hundreds of spec homes that Gypco planned to build. Martin Henry Investments agreed to provide up to 2,000 lots per year, graded and prepped for foundations. Our new company spent millions of dollars securing land for Gypco to purchase.

With proceeds from the sale of Seppala & Aho in South Carolina, Nancy and I surprised all 26 sons and daughters. We presented each one a slice of God's blessing: $50,000. In retrospect, I wish I had carved off larger helpings for each one — good fortune can tumble as quickly as it rises.

While Martin Henry's millions simmered within huge parcels of land, the national housing and credit markets abruptly "boiled over." For a decade, banks had been handing out wads of cash to borrowers with poor or *no* credit history. In this fresh economic downturn, businesses began laying off workers, and homeowners could no longer afford to pay their mortgages. Foreclosures swamped the lenders. To offset their losses, loan officers abruptly altered their liberal lending policies to "cherry-pick" only the borrowers with sizeable equity that could easily be liquidated.

Gypco broke faith with us, simply walking away from their commitment to build homes on thousands of lots we were paying for. They likely tiptoed close to bankruptcy, like so many other construction companies. They "paid" us for work we had

A thoroughly lived life

completed with vacant parcels of land rather than cash.

This era is known historically as the "subprime mortgage crisis." It was a period when the bank manager became "Caesar" in the business arena. Caesar commanded the power to condemn small businesses with a single gesture. Martin Henry Investments fought hard to stay alive, but the time came when we had to restructure loans as they matured. Without warning, our colleagues in commercial banking refused to refinance our projects. Caesar pointed "thumbs down."

After years of improper lending, red ink flooded banks. To wring out every last dime of equity, Caesar targeted Martin Henry Investments, along with thousands of other small companies.

We rushed to finish up projects. Our sales team had clients ready to buy from us, and we juggled hundreds of loan payments to keep them up-to-date.

But Caesar called in loans, anyway, foreclosing before we could complete sales transactions. To help them survive, we dug deep into our pockets to pay off the small subcontractors who had worked for us.

In the end, we lost Martin Henry Investments.

"Loss" is a taskmaster with whom I have never shared my life *comfortably.*

I have grieved over four grandchildren who departed to heaven before me — I miss them dearly. I've lost my first wife, Barbara, and my beloved firstborn son, Sep (Daniel), to cancer. At 85, my own chemotherapy and radiation cancer treatments forced me to shift to a lower gear for a time. My heart beats with "mechanical" assistance these days as well.

Like processing vats of maple syrup, my dreams have been rendered down to a *cupful.* I had hoped to invest in many new opportunities and ministries, but "… the Lord gave and the Lord hath taketh away. Blessed be the name of the Lord" (Job 1:21). God knows what is best.

The best is yet to come

After this "rendering" of my life and times, a cupful of sweetness remains for others to enjoy with me. I testify that "old age" is nothing to fear, after all. In fact, Jesus has imparted to me the greatest fulfillment I have ever known. Loss is shackled to this earth and can never follow me or my loved ones to heaven. My employment at this time is to submit to God's will daily. He continues to steer my ambitious nature along the narrow path that leads to everlasting life.

Nancy and I have shared joys and trials with our 26 children and 130 grandchildren (at last count). Six of these grandchildren have been rescued from orphanages, "engrafted" into our family tree. I had left unfinished business when I flew out of Moscow in 2000. When my daughter Marcie and Nancy's daughter Janie discussed adopting children, Jesus reminded me of this unfinished business.

I have never been able to erase the faces of those abandoned boys and girls at Russian prisons and orphanages from my mind …

჻჻჻

Janie, Marcie and Nancy clattered in the kitchen, loading the dishwasher after dinner. I sat in the living room, enjoying a good chat with their husbands, Cliff and Luke.

I was so proud of my tenacious children. Cliff and Janie (Somero) and Marcie and Luke (Holombo) were finally summiting the peaks of regulations required to adopt two orphaned "citizens of the Russian Federation."

Both couples had been complying with Russia's strict "Civil Procedure Code" to adopt two boys under the age of 24 months. All American court documents had been certified and translated into Russian, with the translator's signature authenticated. Before the two children could tread on U.S. soil, Janie and Marcie would be required to register with the local

A thoroughly lived life

Russian consular's office. Russian monitors examined the living conditions for the children, and the Somero and Holombo families promised to allow other inspections in the future.

After months of red tape, Janie, Marcie and their husbands were declared "fit" to raise Russian children. The two boys still resided in an orphanage in Kazan, Russia, but their rooms in South Carolina were decorated, chest-of-drawers stuffed with tees and footie pajamas. At baby showers, friends and family generously supplied toddler shoes and socks, pull-toys, diapers, wipes and colorful boyish outfits as gifts.

For weeks, Janie and Marcie jumped at every ring of the telephone, expecting to receive a go-ahead from the orphanage to collect their baby sons. One day, after a family dinner at our home, the deciding call came from the adoption agency. Janie and Marcie set the phone on speaker and headed to our bedroom.

Our girls looked crestfallen as a woman unemotionally declared that their two boys simply were "no longer available." No explanation.

Before the agency official hung up, she said, "But, we do have two *girls* who have been cleared for adoption."

To expect a mother and father to *replace* a baby (affixed to their hearts) with a "new" one is akin to emotional torture. Our daughters and their husbands were crushed. Should they reconsider adopting children from Russia?

Nancy and I could do little to comfort our daughters, except to pray for them. By God's grace, each couple reclaimed their resolve, deciding to rescue whomever the Lord Jesus chose for their families.

They traded boys' clothing for girls' clothing at the malls, preparing for daughters instead of sons. Then the Kazan orphanage called *once again* with disappointing news. The two baby girls who had supplanted the boys (in all of our hearts) were suddenly unavailable!

The best is yet to come

Only God's power kept us from yielding to bitterness against the merciless Russian bureaucracy. And how could we trust this adoption official, who assured us that now two beautiful Russian boys awaited the families at Kazan?

Nancy and I bought tickets and accompanied Cliff, Janie, Marcie and Luke to Zurich, then Moscow. Our Russian guide and translator, Kosta, helped us settle into the Hotel Sovietski, outside of Moscow, and we wearily gathered together in one of our rooms to talk over our train schedule. Our conversations drifted toward our experience with the Russian bureaucracy, and Kosta waved his hands in alarm. He lifted up a flower vase to point out a "bug." We read the message in his fearful eyes: Americans were still considered enemies in Russia.

The next day we left the Moscow train depot aboard Pullmans, probably much like the first railcars that clattered in the American West at the turn of the century. Hard benches of worn leather afforded passengers uncomfortable seating. We slept atop wooden bunks in cramped compartments. I was the only one hungry enough to stomach the cuisine of biscuits and liver sausage offered to passengers.

Before the train reached the city of Kazan, our Pullmans jostled past countless poverty-stricken residents bundled up, walking the streets. We passed long stretches of uncultivated fields and dreary, unpainted buildings, most of which seemed vacant.

At our hotel, a few miles from the orphanage, Kosta spent several minutes speaking to a desk clerk to check us in. We were advised not to leave the hotel without escort, due to rampant, violent crime in the area. While carrying our luggage upstairs, Kosta informed us to shower quickly during the one hour of rationed hot water each day. The hotel boiler was finicky, so we wore coats all evening in our rooms.

The next overcast morning, Kosta called for a van, and the seven of us crowded inside with a little suitcase full of extra

A thoroughly lived life

clothing and diapers to care for our two boys on the trip home — God willing. My stomach churned from strange food and worry over the final stages in the adoption process. I could only imagine what the four prospective parents were feeling.

We stopped on a street beside an imposing block building, and Kosta escorted us into a sterile office with a massive metal desk.

Eunice, the bespectacled gray-haired orphanage director, in his late 50s, said in broken English, "Welcome, my American friends."

He seemed to be genuinely glad to see us and extended his hand to Cliff, Luke and me. Eunice handed Kosta the final forms, and he translated them for us. We paid Eunice's fee in rubles, and he nodded with satisfaction. It seemed that every "T" had been crossed and every "I" dotted properly. He slid the rubles and forms into a drawer.

"The children are coming," he said, and no sooner had he spoken than two women carrying the boys entered the room.

Luke and Marcie gently embraced thin, pale Rye, tears in their eyes. Cliff and Janie hugged their tiny son, Hayden. Eunice watched thoughtfully and spoke to Kosta who translated: "Perhaps there's a God after all … these children look so very much like their new parents."

Upon leaving the orphanage, can you guess who among our weary band took away the choicest blessing of the day? I'm sure it was Grandpa Marty and Grandma Nancy. Rye glued himself to Marcie's side, and Hayden nestled close to Janie.

We had one more legal hurdle to master so that Rye and Hayden could leave Russia behind. Someros and Holombos were required to present their children to a Moscow judge for an inspection. It seemed to be a final opportunity to show us Americans the power of the Russian State. In a Moscow courtroom, Kosta interpreted the judge's practiced recitation, and we left after signing more documents.

The best is yet to come

Rye and Hayden had lived in a clinical, regimented environment consisting of crib, exercise time, meals and little else. Orphan babies seldom cried — no one paid attention if they did. Cabbage soup was the staple in their diets. Tea replaced milk and formula for infants, and most of the orphans in Kazan suffered from at least mild malnutrition.

As soon as we had control of our two little ones, we searched the stores for baby food, but found little on the shelves. Marcie and Janie couldn't wait to get the boys home to strengthen them on fine Finnish fare. We all rolled into South Carolina, worn out but fulfilled, our God-inspired mission accomplished.

A year later, Cliff, Janie, Nancy and I faced another nerve-racking foray into Russian territory. We flew back to Moscow and took the same train to the orphanage in Kazan to pick up our 22-month-old grandson, Carter. Then a few months later, Luke and Marcie flew to collect our baby granddaughter Jayce.

Cliff and Janie knew the bureaucratic ropes pretty well by the time they flew their last trips to Russia in 2004 to rescue our granddaughter Karis; then again in 2006 to carry home our little Kate.

సాఖ్యౖ

"Let's pump water and saw wood! Do you know that Jesus loves you?"

Little boys all over the world have gripped the playful hand of this old Finn. Near their ages, I cobbled together a preacher's chicken coop, but grew up to build 10-story high-rises and sprawling shopping centers. I pray for their successes, too.

"And you little chickadees! Jesus loves you, too!"

Little girls flock to the warmth of a kind heart. For many of the songbirds on my path, these "seeds" of God's love may be the only ones they've ever tasted.

A thoroughly lived life

At the Kazan orphanage, I remember children holding hands tightly as they played in their exercise yard. They yearned for love and seized affection from anyone in reach.

I stood with Nancy, listening to the orphans chattering, when suddenly one 3-year-old boy broke away from the group and ran to me. I leaned down, and he hugged me with all his might, soaking in a grandfather's compassion, if only for a moment.

If I could have taken *all* of these unwanted kids home with me to America, I would have.

I've learned that, sometimes, a man's drive to succeed can distract him from life's priorities. Annie Seppala, my mother and spiritual mentor, spent lonely years at the Rindge farm after my father's death. In those frantic days, my new bride, my babies and my business swamped me. It saddens me now that young Marty never expressed how he really felt. His words, "I love you," would have imparted joy to his mother's heart.

God NEVER fails to say that he loves us. Jesus kneels down and opens his arms wide with mercy to every person. When we repent (change our direction) and believe (follow him with all our hearts), his gentle Spirit urges us "orphans" to become part of his heavenly family forever.

I celebrate every "adopted" son and daughter that I have invited to join God's family during many years of preaching. An inheritance of eternal life awaits each one! (John 3:16, Romans 8:14-16).

❧❧❧

Before I perform a wedding ceremony, Nancy and I invite the engaged couple for a cup of coffee and counseling. I speak frankly to them, reflecting on my own "Thoroughly Lived Life." Nancy and I urge a couple to:

The best is yet to come

- Tell their partners "I love you" many times a day.
- Pray together, especially before dropping off to sleep.
- Compliment one another often, to bolster confidence.
- Attend church on time without fail.
- Settle on who handles money most efficiently, and share financial decisions.
- Ask forgiveness from God and one another for shortcomings.
- Be forgiving.

These seven habits keep the foundation level, upon which newlyweds can build strong Christian homes.

In this 86th year of my "Thoroughly Lived Life," I still set the tone of every new relationship with a heartfelt expression: "I'm the happiest man in the world! And do you know why? Because I have the best wife in the world, and I am going to heaven when I die!"

Nancy and I live like migrating birds these days, between warm nests in South Carolina and Florida. At either home, our family gathers often.

Doctors in both communities fuss and tinker with me, keeping my organs operating at peak performance, and Nancy pampers me, too.

Our lives continue to revolve around the Apostolic Lutheran Church, which has kept us mindful of heaven during our sojourn on earth. Nancy and I are able to sponsor spontaneous Bible studies with friends in our neighborhood. We lift our praises to Jesus, with Nancy's skillful accompaniment on the piano.

I enjoy being an elder, and I sense my affection for worldly prosperity loosening its intense grip on my mind. Some of my pressing responsibilities in ministry I've passed on to younger men whom I know.

A thoroughly lived life

But my youthful ambitions still roar inside this aging frame. I hear echoes of myself sitting in Uncle Bill's Model A, saying, "I'm goin' to build things, and I'll have a big store and 'bout 300 trucks!"

Perhaps it's time to grab the bull by the horns and *expand* again — this time in oil-rich Texas! A few Finns I know are ready to throw in their lots with me ...

Do it now? Nancy may have something to say about this. And I might have to listen this time.

A multi-millionaire asked me once, "Marty, how can I take my wealth with me to heaven? There must be a way ..."

I explained that the only thing he could *take* to heaven would be his desire to worship and serve Jesus. It's all he would ever need for eternity!

My challenge until the day I die will be to keep greed from distorting my own God-given ambition. I have seen greed corrupt many good men. Only God can judge how well I have done. I've purposely placed myself and my business under the scrutiny of Godly men I respect. Often Jesus himself guided me past hidden moral or ethical snares.

I pray that I have left a legacy of *trust* in my wake. As a minister of the gospel of Jesus Christ, I have endeavored to give more than was expected.

ॐ ॐ ॐ

These days, I recollect my past life in vivid, colorful vignettes, but I don't live there. I glimpse scenes of my destiny, but eternity stretches far beyond my comprehension. In awe of my past *and* unfathomable future, I close the book and reflect awhile.

Curiously, what is most important to me at this moment *is this moment.* I treasure one earthly asset above homes, bank accounts or all my achievements to date: TIME.

The best is yet to come

I need *time* to be certain every family member is ready to join Nancy and me for a great reunion in heaven. I am jealous of each moment God grants me, to tell everyone I meet that Jesus loves him or her.

It comforts me to know that God is still composing every detail of my "Thoroughly Lived Life." Death is simply a page I'll turn in order to read the next exciting chapter.

The best is yet to come.

Nancy and Marty
Wedding picture
December 2, 1983

Nancy and Marty
cutting the wedding
cake

Girls singing at the wedding.
Marty's: Millie (13), Marci (14), Mindy (16)
Nancy's: Alice (16), Janie (14), Norma (11)

Nancy and Marty at
the beach

May 28, 1995, Confirmation class, Apostolic Lutheran
Church, Greer, South Carolina.
Darrin Clark, Ryan Seppala, Joshua Sarkela,
Marty Seppala, Patti Sauvola, Wendy Seppala,
Linda Niemela, Misty Kinnunen

Martin Seppala Family, September 1995
Back Row: Josh, Annie, Daniel, Nathan, Samuel, Joel,
Benjamin, Mindy, Marty
Middle Row: Heidi, Millie
Front Row: Matthew, Marci, Sandy, Amos, Debbie, Wanda,
Jonathan

Marty's Model A - Marty, Cappy (new puppy) and Nancy

Marty parasailing at 80 years old with Nancy.

Fishing in Alaska. Nancy with her Red Salmon.

Marty catches big King Salmon.

Sarkela Family. Back Row: Bruce, Steve, John, Rodney, David
Front Row: Norma, Alice, Janie, Naomi, Nancy

Marty and Nancy

Sisters and Brothers, February 2008
Back Row: Alvina, Arnold, Elaine
Front Row: Marty, Wally, Edwin

Loving Daughters: Millie, Marty, Wanda

Marty's Girls: Heidi, Debbie, Millie, Annie, Marty, Nancy, Sandy, Marci, Wanda, Mindy

Martin Seppala Family Reunion, Pigeon Forge, TN, June 2011
Back Row: Josh, Joel, Matthew, Millie, Wanda, Sandy, Heidi, Nathan, Benjamin, Samuel
Front Row: Amos, Debbie, Annie, Nancy, Martin, Mindy, Marci, Jonathan

Marty and Nancy, Thanksgiving Day, 2011
Healthy and happy - the best is yet to come!

Conclusion

Writing my memoirs was an emotional journey for me. I have realized how the Lord has led me throughout my whole life, showing grace and mercy in every situation. This journey has shown me that the shortcomings in my life have been covered so completely with Jesus' blood that I have lived a fulfilled and joyful life.

My hope would be for every reader to be a partaker of this wonderful contentment that only Jesus can provide. Our happiness comes only with God's peace in our heart and not with fame or fortune.

My prayer is that every reader will come to know that heaven is his home: The best is yet to come!

Postscript

My heart is full ... of children!

Daniel, my firstborn son, ran our family business in later years, and when Barbara and I moved to Florida, he lived at our memorable home we called Wind Swept Acres, in Rindge. Charismatic and selfless, he made each of us feel special. His wonderful wife, Judy, grieved with us when he died of lung cancer at 56 years old.

Our eldest daughter, Sandy, has always gathered children to her like a mother hen. Ambitious, with a ready smile, she has inherited her father's drive. She married a kind, hospitable man who opens his home to family and friends. Cal is Sandy's perfect match.

Quiet and thoughtful, our Annie married young and raised a large family, like Barbara and I. Steve, her husband, is a well-known entrepreneur, helpful to those in need. You'll find Annie and Steve feeding the homeless at local soup kitchens. Family can't wait for invitations to enjoy their elegant home with them.

All the guys flocked around Debbie when she was a girl. An organized and spotless homemaker, she sometimes cried when our grimy boys messed up the house. Now her own home is beautiful, and with Lloyd, her husband, they entertain guests with enthusiasm and grace. And the food! They serve Lloyd's special berries from the vines he cultivates.

Grampa Marty and Gramma Nancy love to visit Sam, Ruthie and the kids in New England. Sam owns his own construction business: Seppala Construction, in Rindge. His own sons work for him, and I have passed the "Scepter of the Spatula" to Sam: Now he makes blueberry pancakes for everyone.

The best is yet to come

I felt so proud of my son Jonathan, who graduated early and studied for his general contractor's license in Florida. He was the boy who would pick up the trash when others kicked it out of the way. Jon and his wife, Rita, lost their 5-year-old son, Micah, to cancer, and Gramma Nancy and I were present at Children's Hospital when he went home to be with Jesus.

"I love everyone in the whole wide world!" Our daughter Wanda would spread her arms wide when she said it. She married Dave Aho, and he and I converse in Finnish, the language of our fathers. Their children, grandchildren and other family members live near them and visit often. Wanda hasn't changed: Her love truly makes everyone feel welcome.

Our son Joey discovered a gem of a wife. Sheelah loves music, and her children love Grampa and Gramma! Joey inherited my independent spirit and runs his own business. Whether playing guitar or singing for youth groups and conventions, Joey and Sheelah joyfully serve God.

Nathan married young, and he, too, walks in his father's footsteps with a large family. Dozens of employees look to him for paychecks, and his wife, Joan, runs the house like a fine Swiss watch. Nate and Joan are blessed with the gift of hospitality, and seldom is their home empty of guests.

Our heavy-equipment jockey in the family is Benjamin, who started a family young with his first wife, Kathy. She passed away with leukemia, and God gave him a wonderful helpmate and mother for his kids: Tiffany. Our Benny and Tiffany have raised their children together and face life like two peas in a pod.

Our "carefree" entrepreneur, Matthew, fell in love with Mindy, and Mindy *loved* children, which is just what our boy needed! As a fun-loving couple, they adopted kids along with their own. Through the trials of losing two of their precious ones, they are examples to all of us for their faith in Jesus, the One who invites us to seek him, like sons and daughters.

Postscript

Music has been Heidi's gift to her family. As a wonderful pianist, she inherited an appreciation of music from Barbara. We love our Heidi dearly, and good music follows her into every room. I think her heart reaches out to God through every note she plays.

What can I say about Amos? He agreed to come to South Carolina and work with me, in an unproved venture. For several years we worked side-by-side, and he branched off on his own to open a plumbing business. His sweet Jana always welcomed us to their home, where a Bible sits on the kitchen table, the centerpiece for their home.

As a schoolboy, my son Josh aced all his classes. He, too, worked with me in South Carolina in the good old (hard old) days and married Alice, Nancy's daughter, a beautiful girl. If you stop by, the first thing they ask is, "Can you stay for dinner?" And if you know anything about Alice's cooking, you do!

An active child — that was our Mindy. Her husband, Tomas, married an entrepreneur every bit as ambitious as I am. She builds houses while Tomas pastors a church in South Carolina. His roots go deep in Finnish soil, and he and Mindy manage life with faith and grace that few can understand. Their beloved daughter, Moriah, went to be with Jesus and waits for them to come home, too.

Marci praises Jesus with a beautiful voice, inherited from her mother. Marci's talents range far and wide, including interior decorating — and choosing a wonderful husband. Luke and Marci have adopted two Russian children who will always have a Christian home and loving parents.

Millie, our last and the happy daughter, was the "popular" teen and has always invited friendships with her sweet spirit. She is easy to love and has a gift of having a wonderful time in most any circumstance. Her children are blessed to have a mother who thinks "young" — much like their Grampa Marty.

The best is yet to come

Two stepdaughters whom I walked down the aisle of matrimony:

Norma, Nancy's youngest daughter, turned 11 years old on the day we married. Responsible and independent, Norma married an equally ambitious young man. Benji and Norma tied the knot right after she graduated high school. With her servant's heart, Norma has the God-given ability to get along with almost anyone.

Janie was 14 years old when Nancy and I married. Respectful and organized, Janie married a fine Christian man, Cliff Somero. Cliff and Janie adopted four children from Russia. Nancy and I accompanied Cliff and Janie (along with Luke and Marci, who adopted two children) to Russia to bring their children home. These days, we stay with Cliff and Janie when we sojourn in South Carolina.

Contact Information

Marty and Nancy Seppala
can be reached at the following:

1063 Andrew Redding Road
Lantana, Florida 33462

561-588-9801

E-mail: nancyseppala@aol.com

To find out more about leaving a lasting legacy,
please contact Good Book Publishing at
www.goodbookpublishing.com

GOOD BOOK
PUBLISHING

www.goodbookpublishing.com